Manchester United

The Insider Guide

Dedicated to all United fans around the world

Contents

the insider guide

Manchester United The

Insider Guide

Welcome to the 100%
official book where
United stars reveal
the secrets of life at
Old Trafford in their
own words...

Man Un

ited
the insider guide

**by Justyn Barnes
and Sam Pilger**

Thanks to
The players and staff at Manchester United
Lou Pepper
James Freedman
Nicky Paris
Anna Kiernan
Tim Forrester
Adam Bostock
Emma Hughes
Gemma Thompson
Hans Lokoy
Andy Mitten
Rachel Jervis
Craig South
Esther McAuliffe
Faith Mowbray
Martin Norris

Design
Carol Briggs

The Insider photographer
John Peters

Other photos
Rob Wilson
Frank Spooner Pictures
Jay Brooks
Silje Langvaer
Action Images
Sportshot
Prosport
Allsport
Manchester Evening News
Empics
Mark Leech

Video grabs
Creative Convergence

First published in 1997 by
Manchester United Books
an imprint of
VCI plc
72–74 Dean Street,
London, W1V 5HB

in association with
**Manchester United
Football Club plc**
Old Trafford, Manchester,
M16 ORA

CIP data for this title is
available from the British
Library

ISBN 0 233 99340 1
Produced by **Zone Ltd**

Printed in France

ICE
BERG

Henning Berg is so cool on the pitch you'd think he has ice in his veins, but would he collapse under our Insider spy's interrogation? Not a bit of it. This Norseman is so laid back, he's horizontal...

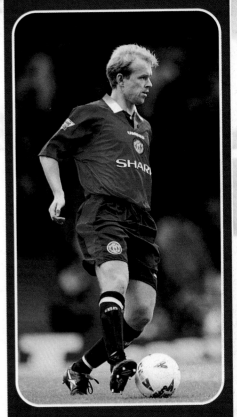

Will you stay living in Blackburn while you play for Manchester United?
No, we have just found a new house in Wilmslow and we're moving there shortly. It is better for Hilde to be nearer to the girlfriends of the other Norwegians at the club.

How is life in England?
Lovely. I have been enjoying my time here. On the footballing side, things have gone well and that is important. My family are happy here as well, we are settled.

Is there anything you think is strange about the English way of life?
Not really, life in England is quite similar to how we live in Norway. I guess that is one of the reasons why Norwegian players settle so quickly when they come over here.

What do you miss most about Norway?
Nothing really, except our friends and family. I go to Norway regularly to meet up with the national team, so there's nothing I really get to miss. Again, life in England is not very different. And we get Norwegian newspapers and watch Norwegian TV via our satellite dish.

Are you married?
Yes, I have been married to Hilde for two years. We have been together for much longer; she moved to England with me five years ago. We have an 11-month-old son, William.

When you finish your career in England, will you go back to live in Norway?
Definitely, yes. We want our son William to grow up in Norway and we have roots there with family and old friends.

What is your favourite music?
I listen to a lot of different music. It's difficult to pinpoint any particular favourites, as there are so many. Since I came over to England I've listened to a number of English bands which are brilliant although unknown in Norway. I don't buy lots of CDs but I listen to the radio a lot during the day.

What is your favourite food?
Again, no particular preferences. But I enjoy a good meal, whether it is at home with Hilde or going out to a restaurant.

And TV?
I watch a lot. My favourites would probably be sports programmes, football matches...

What's the last film you went to see?
I remember that vividly, because it was yesterday. We don't go to the cinema often as we need a baby-sitter for William. But we did go last night and it turned out to be the worst film I have ever seen. It was *Speed 2*.

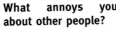

I usually prefer action films, but this one was horrendous.

And your favourite book?
I rarely read books, and when I do it's usually fiction or crime books. I like Jan Guilluo, a Swedish writer. I think I have read most of his works.

What other sports do you play?
When I was younger I used to go skiing a lot and at school I specialized in sports so I played a lot of different things.

When did you get your first pair of football boots?
Oh, my memory is letting me down again! I started playing for a team when I was seven or eight years old, so it must have been around that time.

Best Christmas present ever received?
Here we go again... I haven't a clue, don't remember... (thinks long and hard) Possibly a car racing track when I was a little kid.

Who was your childhood football hero?
No one in particular, actually. United was my favourite club but I didn't have any individual heroes. There were many good United players around, like Steve Coppell, Bryan Robson and later Jesper Olsen, but I wouldn't say they were my heroes.

What annoys you about other people?
I am a very tolerant and nice person, so I can put up with almost anything. I don't get easily worked up.

How do you relax?
By doing as little as possible. Since we had William, I have found that playing with him is great relaxation. Otherwise I just listen to music or watch the TV.

Describe yourself in five words.
That's too many! Can we keep it down to two or three? Hmmm, I am probably honest, single-minded (when it come to football) and a quite kind person. Those three are enough!

What's your advice for young footballers who want to make it to professional?
Don't think too much about your ambitions. Instead, concentrate on developing your skills, enjoying football. If you can improve your shooting, tackling and dribbling enough while having fun, then maybe you'll make it.

What's your best moment in football so far?
Winning the League with Blackburn in 1995 must be the best. And qualifying for the World Cup with Norway then beating Mexico in the first match.

Do you have any family pets?
No, but my family had a dog called Boy when I was younger.

Do you cook?
Yes, I do spring a surprise occasionally. It would probably be chicken and chips – no, just kidding. I can make meat balls or some other Norwegian dish. We try to eat some traditional Norwegian food, lots of fish for instance.

Are you very domesticated?
Not really, but I try to do my share. I am quite handy with the vacuum cleaner and I look after William a lot so Hilde can tend to other things.

Is there any job you absolutely refuse to do?
Too many! I hate washing the floor and dusting.

Do you do the weekly shopping?
Hilde usually takes care of that, but I have been seen at Sainsbury's every now and then!

Describe your ideal day at home.
Coming home from training to play with William, watch a good football match, maybe enjoy a good meal with Hilde. That would be a good day.

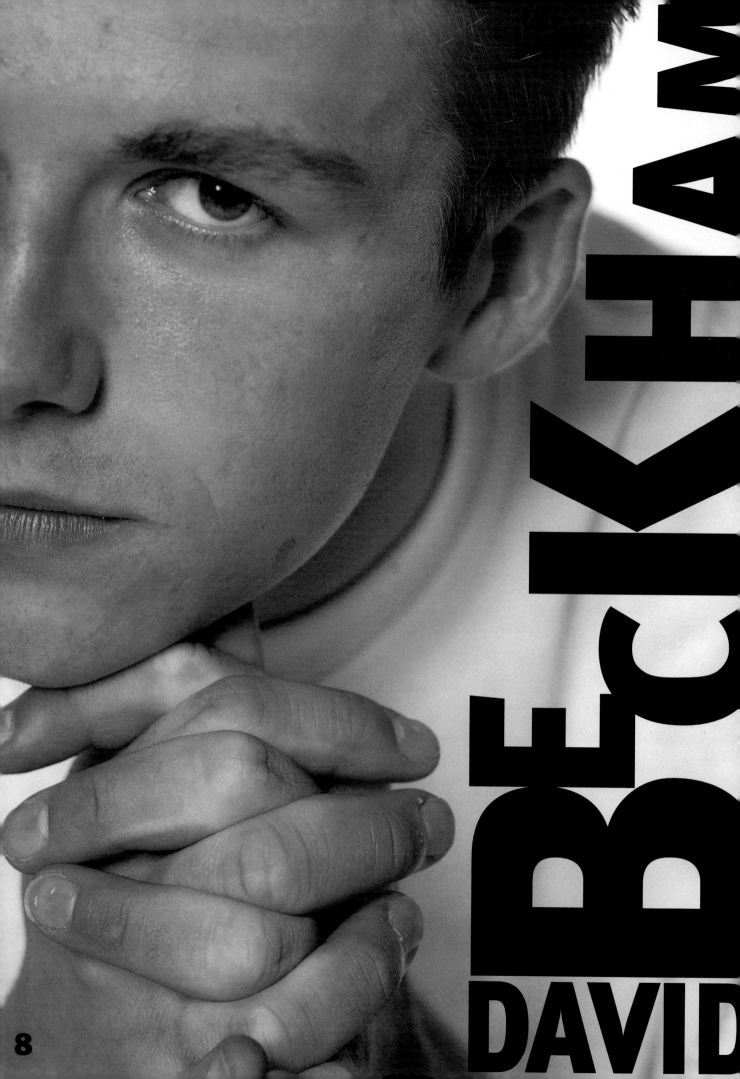

BECKHAM

DAVID

"From day one, his talent had to be seen to be believed. There's no doubt he will go on to become one of the most dominant players in English football," said United youth coach Eric Harrison in 1995. In just two years, David Beckham has fulfilled Harrison's prophecy.

A Nineties football icon, Beckham has made an effortless transition from a promising youngster to Manchester United and England regular in just 18 months. "Some mornings I wake up and pinch myself to make sure that all this is happening to me," says David. "Everything seems to have happened so fast.

"Life has definitely changed. I've been on the front pages of the newspapers. Last year I could walk down the street and not be noticed. This year, I've got people coming up to me all the time. I have my picture taken when I walk around Manchester or when I come out of a restaurant. But it's a small price to pay when you consider what I have got out of soccer."

Born in Leytonstone in 1975, David always wanted to be a footballer and to play for Manchester United. His United-supporting dad Ted was behind him all the way. "I was at Arsenal and Tottenham, one day a week each, and I could have signed for either of them. But I always wanted to play for Man United, because I supported them since I was young." David even wore a United shirt to his trial at Tottenham.

"I got some publicity for winning the Bobby Charlton skills competition when I was 11, but United first noticed me when I was playing for my district team. A scout called Malcolm Fidgeon came over to my mum and asked if I would like to come to Old Trafford."

Eric Harrison, the United youth team coach, remembers the young David well. "I knew as soon as I saw him in action that he had the natural ability to make a really big name for himself," Eric recalls. "The one worry I had about him was that he was so tiny and skinny. But Mother Nature lent a hand. In a year, David must have grown eight inches and put on two stone. You don't need me to tell you what a talent he has developed in to."

"Leaving home at only 16, I was homesick for the first month or two, but you get used to it once you start playing," says David. "The worst time is when you're not playing, and that's when I missed home the most. I was lucky to have some brilliant digs. I lived in three different ones, but I liked the third one best. They had Mark Hughes there before me."

David made his first-team debut in October 1992, coming on as a substitute in a League Cup tie at Brighton. He had to wait over two years for another chance, this time in the Champions' League clash with Galatasaray. Gary Neville and Nicky Butt had already played for the first team, but there was talk that the finest of Fergie's fledglings, David Beckham, was yet to show himself. And he proved it against the Turks by giving an accomplished performance and scoring.

In the spring of 1995, Ferguson loaned out David to Preston North End. He remembers his time in the Third Division fondly. "It was one of the best months of my career and I owe a lot to them. My stay there gave me loads of confidence. In about four games, I scored three goals and was awarded Man of the Match a few times too. At United, everything is done for you – even your kit is laid out. Whereas at Preston, you have to take your kit home and wash it yourself, which I wasn't used to at all!"

With the departures of Ince and Kanchelskis, David was given his chance in midfield at the beginning of the 1995/96 season. He made the most of it, playing 32 times and scoring eight goals. Dismissed on the first day of the season as being too young, by the end of the season David had picked up a Championship medal and an FA Cup winners' medal. "It did annoy me and the other younger players a little bit, but when people said we couldn't win the

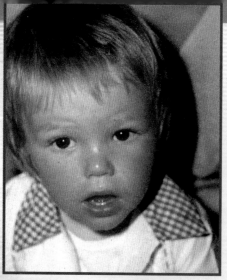

"His passing is his talent. He sees the farthest man first. There's plenty around who see the nearest first. If you can see the farthest, and then come back from there, your options are better."
GLENN HODDLE

League, we loved it. Look how we responded. It was satisfying to prove all our critics wrong and become Champions."

The following season promised much for David and he started it as he meant to go on with his unforgettable halfway line goal against Wimbledon on the opening day of the season.

"That goal" started the David Beckham phenomenon. He was everywhere, on magazine covers and on billboards, as the fresh new face of English soccer. The tabloid press followed his every move. It was news if he wore glasses or didn't wear socks. And of course there was the question of who he was dating.

"I've had a lot of stick off the lads in the dressing room," laughs David. "The young prominent players have always got that here; Lee Sharpe got it and Giggsy

before me. When things are written in the papers about you, you have to expect the lads to give you some grief."

On the field, he continued to prosper. The autumn of 1996 saw a breathtaking string of goals from outside the area against Derby, Liverpool, West Ham, Tottenham and Nottingham Forest. David also began to take responsibility for United's creative influence. Glenn Hoddle must have seen something of himself in young David who, like Hoddle, had the ability to hit endless, accurate long passes. Hoddle

brought David into the England squad and he was to feature in all of the World Cup qualifiers.

"It can be hard for me to keep my feet on the ground," admits David. "But I have a lot of people here to help me. I don't think I've changed. I always listen to my parents and they will always be there for me. I've also had advice from people like Gary Pallister, Steve Bruce, Bryan Robson and, of course, the manager.

"It does go through my mind what it would be like not to be famous, but I couldn't be happier than I am now. I've got a lovely family, I'm playing for the best club in the world and I've got my own house and car. I never dreamed of having all of this at 22."

BECK'S FIVE FAVES

1 Fave book?
I start a lot of books, but never finish them. I enjoyed one on the Krays though.

2 Fave mags?
I read both *Manchester United* and *Glory Glory Man United* and also *GQ* occasionally.

3 Fave meal?
Chicken or Beef stir-fry. It's gorgeous and I can cook it myself. I hate parsnips and black pudding.

4 Fave music?
Soul music like Stevie Wonder and R Kelly. I like George Michael as well.

5 Fave car?
Porsche 911 Carrera 2S

BECKS' BIG SHOT

"We already had the game won at 2-0 and when I recieved the ball inside my own half. I spotted Wimbledon's keeper Neil Sullivan off his

"I want to be known as a great player. I don't enjoy being on the front pages – I prefer to be on the back."

MY UNITED BEBUT

Champions' League,
v Galatasaray (h), 4–0
7 December 1994

"I found out only an hour and a half before the game that I was playing, so I was a bit nervous. When I scored, the ball travelled to the right of the box. I just hit it and hoped. When I scored, I can't begin to describe the feeling. The first thing I remember is Eric coming towards me. We met in mid-air as I jumped to celebrate – I've got the picture on my wall. Both my parents were at Old Trafford that night. My mum was in tears and my dad shot out of his seat and accidentally head-buttted a bloke next to him."

line and I thought: 'Why not, let's have a go'. It's one of those goals that I will look back on in a few years time and think, 'Did I really do that?'"

"I don't dislike
journalists, it's
more a case of
me not liking
to do inter-
views. I am
quite shy!"
**PAUL
SCHOLES**

THE FAME GAME

**By far Britain's biggest and most
glamorous club, Manchester United
are always back page (and often
front-page) news. Whether Fergie's
signing another star player, Becks
goes shopping with Posh Spice or
Keano shouts at someone, the media
are watching the Reds' every move...**

"I don't think many
journalists have played
pro football. They don't
realise what it's like."
DAVID MAY

"When you play for a big club like United, people are going to knock you, but once again we had the last laugh by winning the championship.
Actions speak louder than words."
ROY KEANE

"I've been linked with girls in the paper that I've never even met! People read these stories and it stays in their minds, even if it's not true."
DAVID BECKHAM

"It's not the money that changes you, or the success and fame, but the media and what they put in the paper. Some people have a picture of what it's like to be famous, and sometimes it's not like that at all.
RYAN GIGGS

"I feel sorry for Ronny Johnsen. He plays superbly week-in, week-out, while I get most of the credit. Even if I'm the worst player on the pitch I still get most of the glory in the Norwegian press."
OLE GUNNAR SOLSKJAER

The pressure of the Premiership can sometimes make even the best go barmy. The players and staff have to do something to unwind, and help to keep the lads relaxed between matches. Our insider photos reveal the side of United that you rarely see in the heat of battle...

ALWAYS REMEMBER

If you are in the dressing room...

feeling hot...

having a stretch...

havin

GOAL KING COLE

One day, Schmikes was feeling a bit low...

so Becks said to Andy, "I bet you'd be useless in goal... "

but Coley laughed and said, "I'll have a go"

Photo magnetic: Becks chuckles up behind Ben

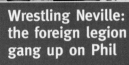

Wrestling Neville: the foreign legion gang up on Phil

Coley goes for the burn

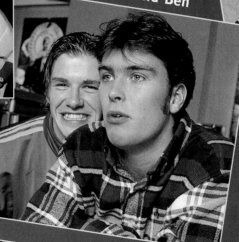

"I am the knight of the onion bag" declares Rai

KEEP YER TONGUE OUT! (Karel never forgets)

or choking on a plane...

nk...

And the lads all chuckled...

when Pob whacked the ball...

but Andy caught it, just like Schmeichel.

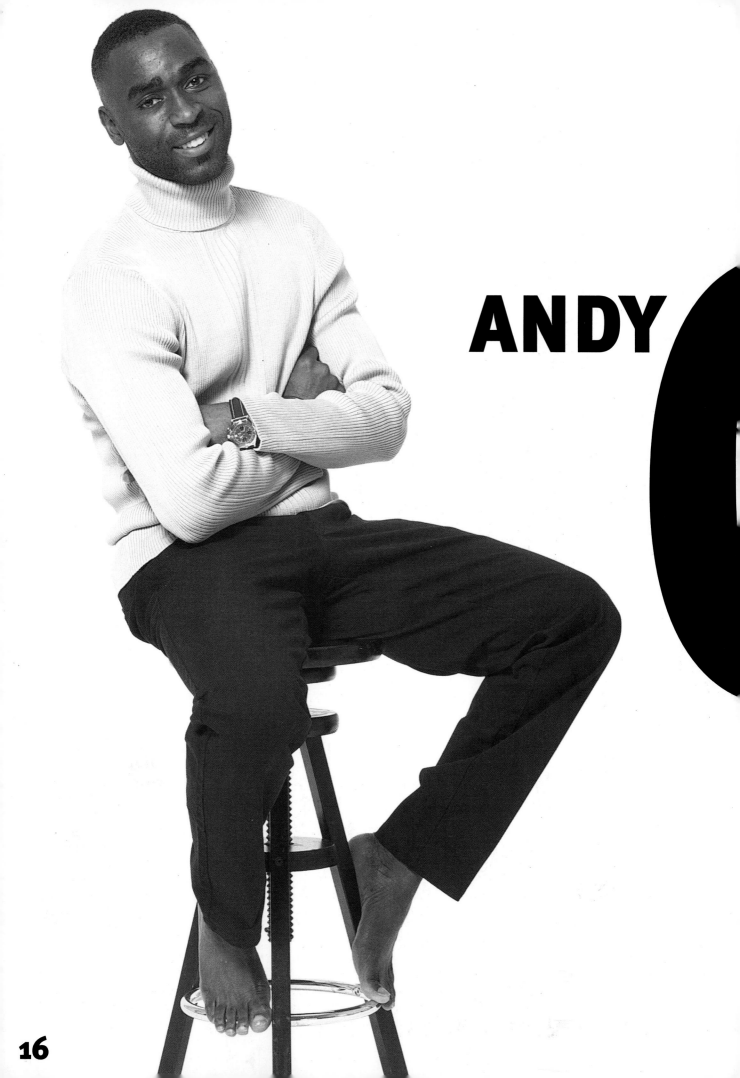

ANDY

OLE

Andy Cole has the best League goalscoring record of any Manchester United striker since Denis Law. Surprised? After all the criticism levelled at him, you would think Andy had not scored for three years. In fact, his goalscoring record is better than any other striker who has played over 50 games for United in the last 25 years – including Cantona, McClair, Hughes, Greenhoff, Jordan and Stapleton.

In his two and a half years at Old Trafford, Cole has averaged a goal every other game. This despite pneumonia, two broken legs and an admitted loss of form during his first season. Andy does not even have the benefit of taking penalties to inflate his record.

"I read somewhere about the 'reviled Andy Cole'. That is rubbish as the fans love him and they know what he is capable of," says Alex Ferguson.

"I have two League Championship medals and a FA Cup winner's medal, so I can't be doing that badly," says Andy. "I was very happy with the way things went when I came back from injury at the beginning of 1997. I proved to myself what I am capable of doing and I was delighted."

Andy started his career at Arsenal in 1989. Although considered an exciting prospect, he had Wright, Smith, Merson and Campbell ahead of him in the queue for striking positions. So after just two games for Arsenal and a loan spell at Fulham, Andy moved on to Bristol City for £500,000. "People thought I was silly to leave Arsenal, but I had a brilliant time at Bristol City. It was a stepping stone to bigger and better things." And so it proved; after 25 goals in just 49 games, Kevin Keegan recruited Andy for £1.75 million to lead Newcastle's charge for promotion.

Andy did not disappoint. He provided the goals that saw Newcastle enter the Premier League as First Division Champions. In his first season in top-flight football, Andy set the record for the most goals scored in a Premiership season with 34 goals (including two against United), a record that still stands today, and collected the PFA Young Player of the Year award.

Andy continued his prolific goalscoring form in his second season with Newcastle in the Premiership, scoring 15 goals. Then in January 1995, Alex Ferguson gave Kevin Keegan a call to pose one simple question: "Is there definitely no way that you would sell me Andy Cole?" Keegan admitted there was and Andy was on his way to Old Trafford for £6.25 million plus Keith Gillespie.

"I got a call from my agent and he said, 'You know you would only leave Newcastle for one club? Well you're going!' I couldn't believe it. Never in my wildest dreams did I expect to join United. I had always been a fan!"

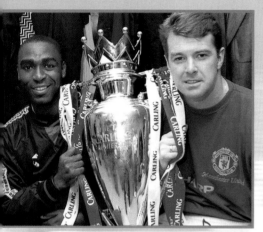

very unfair and really cruel at times. In the end I started to wonder if I really was a bad player, but I knew I was not.

"My family and religion helped me through the low points. I prayed a bit and read the Bible, which was really good. I went through the lowest of lows during my first season here. After a game when I know I've struggled, to come home to my son whizzing around made me realise that there were more important things in life than football. I've got a little boy to bring up."

"I would describe myself as shy. Everyone knows that I keep myself to myself. I'll have a good laugh with the boys but I do like to spend time on my own. I'm a very quiet and shy person until you get to know me."

In his first season at United, Andy scored 12 goals in 16 games, including a record setting five against Ipswich. This despite losing his striking partner, Eric Cantona, after only a game and a half. "It was hard when I first came here, because it was for a lot of money, and when we lost the Championship people said it was because Andy Cole did not score enough goals. I thought: 'What a load of rubbish!'"

He would have to get used to the criticism. The following season, when United won the Double, Andy was often slated in the media. It was true he did not look the same player he had at Newcastle, but as second top scorer and a provider for many others, he played a integral role in the team's success and earned his two medals. There were many highlights: the crucial FA Cup goals against Chelsea and Sunderland, the opener against title rivals Newcastle at Old Trafford and his title-confirming flick at Middlesbrough.

"I tried too hard to justify the fee and too hard to score goals. If I missed, I got down on myself. I was very hurt by all the criticism in my first full season. I was hurting so much inside, you don't know how much. It was

Andy's problems were caused partly by the different system that United played. "I had never played in a system where I play up front on my own and I did find that difficult," he explains. "I like to play with someone else up front because you've always got a chance of getting in. I will always say that for someone to come to United and score 25 to 30 goals will be hard. The goals are

shared out so much at United. The system we play, with one man up front, makes it difficult for one player to score a lot of goals."

Playing in a different system improved Andy's overall game. But to recognise that almost became a cliché to avert attention from his lack of goals. "I thought I contributed a lot to the team. My overall game really improved. The way I play now, I think

MY BEST UNITED GOAL
v Arsenal (a)
19 February 1997

"I really enjoyed this one, it was like my old self. Two touches and the ball was in the back of the net.

'd have scored more goals at ...rdinand and Cole, Andy is by ...ith him. 99 PETER BEARDSLEY

I am a better player. I can do a lot more now than when I came to United from Newcastle. At times, the work elsewhere has been at the expense of scoring. People seem to think that if I'm not scoring then I don't contribute any thing, but I don't agree." During 1996/97, when Andy played only a third of the season, he still managed to contribute eight assists – more than celebrated goal makers such as Giggs and McManaman.

Pneumonia and two broken legs (courtesy of Neil Ruddock in a Reserves game against Liverpool) contrived to wipe out the first half of Andy's season. But he came back to help United to their second successive Championship. His winner against Wimbledon in January sent United to the top of the table and there they remained. His seven goals in 11 games was his best goalscoring run for United, and Glenn Hoddle acknowledged Andy's resurgence in form by recalling him to the England squad after a two-year absence.

Some people seem to feel Andy Cole has been a failure at United, but his scoring record, England caps and three medals say otherwise. "He has come back a better player," said Alex Ferguson. "He has a big future with this club."

TOP TEN UNITED LEAGUE STRIKE-RATES 1973–1997

		Goals	Games	Games per goal
1.	Andy Cole	30	60	2.00
2.	Eric Cantona	64	143	2.23
3.	Stuart Pearson	55	138	2.50
4.	Gordon Hill	39	100	2.56
5.	Mark Hughes	119	345	2.89
6.	Joe Jordan	37	109	2.94
7.	Peter Davenport	22	72	3.27
8.	Frank Stapleton	60	204	3.40
8.	Andrei Kancheslskis	28	96	3.42
9.	Alan Gowling	18	64	3.55
10.	Jimmy Greenhoff	26	94	3.61

MY UNITED DEBUT

**v Blackburn Rovers (h), 1–0
22 January 1995**

"If I'm honest I had butterflies in my stomach, but when I went out there for the warm-up I was okay. The supporters gave me a great welcome. I enjoyed it all, though I was disappointed I didn't score. I had a chance after just 90 seconds. People said it came too

early, but there is never a chance that comes too early."

Gary Neville played a long ball, Tony Adams let it bounce over him and I stole in, nipped it past Lukic and scored."

Gooooaa

United has had some of the finest goal celebration artists down the years – remember the Sharpey Shuffle? Giggsy and Incey used to practice their routines for hours, Eric just had to shrug his shoulders and the crowd went crazy, and Keano's over-the-top celebrations have been known to force goalscorers to go off injured! Here's the insider guide on how to celebrate in true Red style...

1 Over the top
Don't miss out on the fun – jump on top!

2 Schmeichel shimmy
Goalies shouldn't feel left out when the team scores – give it some welly!

3 Group hug
Great for team spirit!

7 The fireman's lift
Put the goalscorer over your shoulder and carry him back to the centre circle

8 Buttster bloodvessel
Clench your fists, open wide and run for the nearest group of fans

aaallll!!!

"I love it when the team scores. The lads are always giving me stick for my over-the-top celebrating, but I'm just so happy I can't help it. One time, Choccy saw me coming, sidestepped my dive, I missed and I did my hamstring!" ROY KEANE

"My 1996 Umbro tournament goal was my first for about four years! Gary said the way I celebrated, you'd have thought I'd scored the winning goal in the Cup Final, not the Umbro Trophy third-place play-off! Every game I tell my Dad I'm going to score; he and my Grandad always have a £5 bet. They've lost a few quid!" PHIL NEVILLE

"Scoring is a mixture of relief and joy. When I celebrate, I'm running so high on adrenalin, I'm not thinking straight and I just do what comes into my head." RYAN GIGGS

4 Striker hug
Show the scorer that you care

5 The first one
You'll never forget your first goal – make sure no one else does!

6 The armchair
Put the squeeze on the scorer with your arms and legs and hang on until they fall over

9 The Keano
Grab 'em round the neck and go over the top!

10 Swing low
Grab his jersey and swing him till he's dizzy

BIG BROTHER

If any footballer has an old head on young shoulders, it's Gary Neville. At 21, Gary was the youngest defender in England's Euro '96 team, but he played like an experienced international. He's totally dedicated to football, and his club and country are reaping the rewards...

FOREVER RED

There are few players as loyal to their club as Gary – for him, United comes first. "I want United to buy the best players in the world, even if they are defenders," he says. "If I can't get in the team, so be it.

"I was a supporter long before I became a player here. When I was an apprentice I sat watching the team with the rest of the fans. I sang my head off, shouted with everyone. It meant so much just to see the club successful.

"In an ideal world, in five years' time, I'd still be at United with about 300 appearances under my belt, 50 England caps, three more Championship medals, a couple of FA Cups winners' medals and a European Cup winners' medal! I really love this club and I never want to leave."

With Becks at the San Siro, Milan

Bleary-eyed on the Big Breakfast

FINE TACKLING

1994/95 was Gary's breakthrough season at United, but his enthusiasm got him into trouble. "I was trying so hard to impress, to let the manager know that I was willing to tackle and get stuck in," remembers Gary. "Maybe I was a little over-exuberant."

Gary's mis-timed tackles meant he reached 40 disciplinary points and faced a ban that could cost him the chance to play in his first FA Cup Final. Although Boss Fergie defended his young star saying, "Gary's an honest lad trying to come to terms with the pace of the Premiership," he still had to face the FA Disciplinary Committee. "It was a bit like walking into the headmaster's office," recalls Gary. "As it happens, I thanked them for being so lenient. Although they did fine me, they could easily have banned me."

Gary was delighted to be available for the Cup Final but he pleaded poverty when he next saw Alex Ferguson. He told the Boss, "I got a lot of those points playing in the Reserves. I was earning Reserve-team wages. I can't afford to pay £1,000." This time Fergie was less sympathetic. "Just wait while I get my handkerchief out Gary," laughed the Gaffer before adding, "You'll need your FA Cup Final win bonus now." United lost 1–0!

FAMOUS FIVE

The Nevilles, Nick, Becks and Scholesy are now major players for United. Previously, four of the five helped to make Boundary Park Juniors probably the best Sunday League side in Britain. "It's frightening to think that just a few years ago, four of us were playing in the Bolton Sunday League," says Gary. "Nicky and me were in midfield with Phil at the back and Paul was striker. We never lost a game in four seasons. David was not even part of the five then, even though I knew him as a friend. Then we all played together in the United Youth teams. Now we're in the first-team squad and we've all played for England. There's a real bond between us."

GAZ'S FIRST GOAL

v Middlesbrough
5 May 1997

For years we held our breath hoping that he'd do it and it finally happened – Gary scored! A pass from Eric

GAZ TALK

1 Making the grade
"My schoolfriends were surprised when I joined United. I hadn't even played for the County side and they must have thought I wasn't good enough. I think playing with better players brought the best out of me."

2 Low profile
"I don't envy Becks and all the limelight he gets. I'm happy being a nice quiet right back who noone wants to talk to."

3 Best friends
"My best friends are Ben Thornley, David Beckham, Chris Casper and Phil, although that's a different sort of relationship."

4 Pre-match nerves
"Before a game I think most people get nervous. But during the game you are concentrating so hard that you don't have time to think about nerves."

5 Long throw-ins
"I've always been able to throw it long. I get a lot of stick from the other lads saying I'm only in the team because of them!"

6 Hero
"Bryan Robson – I was there when he signed for United on the pitch in 1981 and he was my hero after that. When I came to the club he was always there to help."

7 Speakeasy
"I do moan a lot and if I think something isn't right, I will speak up and have a go. Phil often thinks the same as me. It's just that I'm the one who speaks up for both of us."

"I love training"   "Pass the croissants"

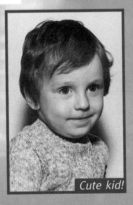
Cute kid!

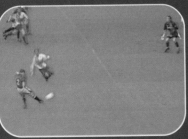

Cantona gave him the chance and Gaz buried it in the onion bag with a ferocious shot. What a buzz!

23

OUR KID

When Gary Neville broke through into the United first team in 1995, it was hard to believe that there was another talented Neville lurking in the Reserves with the same big-match temperament. Since then, Phil, two years Gary's junior, has won the Double and followed his big bruv into the England squad...

GROWING UP

It wasn't simply a matter of age that Phil took a little longer than Gary to establish himself at Manchester United. "Phil was probably the better player at school", remembers Neil Scruton, the headmaster of the Elton High School in Bury which the brothers both attended. The main reason for Phil's slower progress was his equally outstanding talent for cricket which dominated his life between the ages of 11 and 14. "I think Gary wanted to play for United more than me as a youngster," recalls Phil. "I was about 14 when I realised that United was the club for me, too. In his apprentice days, Gary used to come home and tell me about what he'd done and it gave me the taste for it."

Even if Phil was undecided at first, there was no way that United youth coach Eric Harrison was going to let someone of Phil's talent slip away. "Phil stood out from the crowd straight away when he came to the club," says Eric. "Phil got into United's Youth team at the age of

Born to play ball

15. Only the likes of Norman Whiteside and Ryan Giggs have managed that before, so we knew Phil was capable of big things."

Phil's efforts on the football pitch saw his schoolwork suffer. "In my last two years at school, the teachers would let me have the odd day off for United matches. I found it hard to catch up with the work. I got 4 GCSEs, but I don't think my Dad thought any the worse of me for it. I was focused on a career in football."

Eric was impressed by Phil's dedication. "Like his brother, he'll also work until he drops to achieve what he expects and hopes for himself. Phil used to come in and train after school. He was keen as mustard."

Far from being in his brother's shadow when he finally signed for United, Phil has grateful for Gary's good advice. "Gary was really helpful when I joined. He'd tell me what the youth coaches liked and didn't like, so I was always a step ahead." He's stayed ahead ever since.

LOAD OF BAILS

"I think my Dad's dream was for Gary to play for Manchester United and for me to play for Lancashire at Old Trafford cricket ground down the road," says Phil. According to Geoff Ogden, Lancashire CC youth coach, that dream was totally realistic. "Phil was the best left-handed batsman we'd had here since Neil Fairbrother. Phil played for Lancashire Second XI when he was just 15. He made 124 runs for Lancashire Under–15s against Yorkshire and everyone present said it was the best schoolboy innings they'd ever seen. Phil opened the batting; he had textbook technique and a superb temperament. Gary was a terrific batsman too. He played for North Of England Under–15s, but missed England trials

PHIL'S MAGIC FLICK

v Newcastle (h)
8 May 1997

Phil's much more than just a defender. He's as skilful on the ball as he is without it. During this game, against

"It could have been me, Goughie"

Nice thought... not sure about the pic

because of a broken finger." Current England coach David Lloyd hasn't forgotten the Neville brothers either "At 14, they looked head and shoulders above their contemporaries."

BATTING WONDER

● Phil broke the batting records of some famous names. "In the under 13s, I broke Mike Atherton's record of runs in a season. Then in the Under 15s, I beat John Crawley's record too."

● Phil captained England schoolboys at cricket

● Phil's highest score ever was 193 not out for Lancashire in a 50–over match. "I needed eight off my last two balls to get my 200, but I ran my partner out and didn't face the last ball!"

● Neville Neville was a good cricketer and his two sons followed in his footsteps by playing for local side Greenmount Cricket Club. "Dad used to hit for six over the trees and we'd run and fetch it. Gary could do it too, but I couldn't. Gary called me Geoff Boycott because I was a bit defensive. As a left-hander, I liked to think of myself more as David Gower!"

● Phil's Dad used to play with current Aussie captain Mark Taylor at Greenmount CC and Mark came to stay at the Neville's house during the 1997 Ashes series.

"BECKS IN WALKING DOWN THE STREET SHOCKER"

WHY FOOTBALL?

"One week I got picked for England under-15s at both cricket and football," says Phil. "I played football in front of a crowd of 60,000 in the Olympic Stadium, Berlin. I flew home to play cricket for England and there wasn't anyone watching except for the player's families. There just wasn't the same buzz."

"Are you following me?"

Newcastle he out-paced three defenders, before playing an amazing backheel to give Andy Cole a free run on goal...

Ruffle it, just a little bit

For that winning smile

9.00 am "It's a training day so as normal, I get up at about nine, have a wash and shave and clean my teeth before setting off for the trainin ground at about 9.30. I've recently moved into an apartment in Bowdon in Cheshire and it takes about half an hour to get into the Cliff... "

TEDDY SHE

He's the new bloke on the block and Teddy's settling in just fine at Old Trafford. Teddy let our insider photographer follow him on a typical day in the life of a top Premiership footballer. Photocalls, autograph signing and shopping for plates were all on the agenda as Teddy went about his business...

12.15 pm "We finish training at midday, and we all head back to Cliff for a photocall. Have a quick shower and change into the new Champions' League kit. All the lads really like the kit. Apparently it glows in the dark! The goalkeeper's kit is black and looks like it's made out of leather – Schmikes and Rai are well impressed! The photograhers take a team shot and individual pix of all the players too... "

Here I come

Whaddya think of the new kit, Becks?

We gotta run

On the pace

Phil admires my skills!

Time for a slurp

10.30 am "I never eat much before I leave the house because there's tea and toast laid on at the Cliff, so I'll have a bite to eat and chat to the lads before we start training at half past ten. A full English breakfast is not a good idea before Kiddo puts us through our paces anyway. Today we are training at Littleton Road, which backs on to the Cliff, but it's a 10-minute drive away, so I cadge a lift off Becks down there. Contrary to popular opinion, I do enjoy training and you always feel really fit afterwards... "

INGHAM:
a day in the life

Can I have a bite of your apple please Rai?

I'm looking forward to the match, Brian

12.45 pm
"I get changed back into my normal clothes and meet the press in the Cliff car park. Today I'm chatting to a couple of guys from local radio stations, Key 103 and GMR... "

I think the young girl's just seen Giggsy

Plenty of water, not much else!

1.00 pm

"I've been amazed at the support United get. It's still the school holidays and I reckon about a thousand fans come down to the Cliff car park each day and to meet the players and get autographs. I spend about half an hour signing autographs before I set off home... "

1.30 pm

"Get home and find the fridge is empty and the cupboards are bare – typical footballer! I'll have to nip out and do some shopping. I've been so busy since signing for United, that I haven't managed to buy much stuff for my new place, so it's time to hit the local John Lewis.

TEDDY SHERING

Fancy a cup of Rosie Lee?

Ooh, suits you, Sir

4.30 pm

"Time to relax with a nice cup of char. By this time you start to feel a bit tired after training. The Boss likes us to take it easy, and I want to be at my best for the match tomorrow night. I like to play golf but we have to stick to the rules during the season so we are fresh for all the games. No wild night out, tonight! Sit down and read *Arena*, watch a bit of telly and make some phone calls. Although I've brought all this new stuff for the kitchen, I'll probably nip out later for a Chinese takeaway for my dinner – I'm known as the takeaway king!"

The essentials...

...new plates

4.00 pm

"A sucessful trip! I had a bite to eat while I was out and got loads of new crockery and other bits of pieces for the flat, plus a few essentials. The flat still looks a bit bare and I'll still look for a few more bits of furniture to make it more homely."

... saltshaker

HAM: *a day in the life*

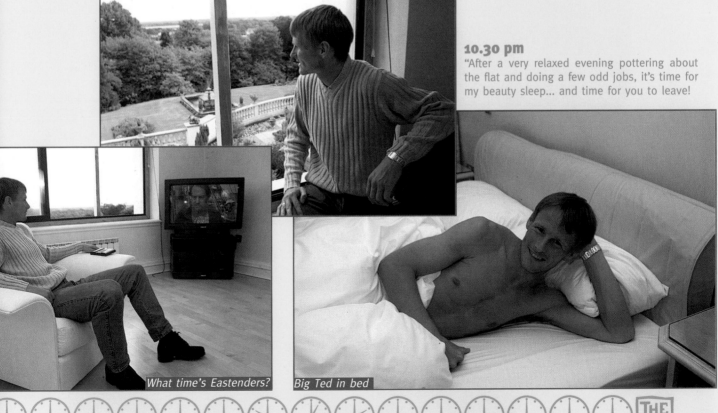

Nice view, eh?

10.30 pm

"After a very relaxed evening pottering about the flat and doing a few odd jobs, it's time for my beauty sleep... and time for you to leave!

What time's Eastenders?

Big Ted in bed

It is six medal-winning years since Ryan Giggs made his debut aged just 17. Every Old Trafford regular has seen moments of sheer Giggs magic, but he still hasn't reached his potential. It's time Ryan took control...

RYAN GIGGS

The mark of the football genius is that he finds doing things other players can only dream of as easy as tying their bootlaces. For example, here's Ryan Giggs' description of one of his most thrilling goals ever, a zig-zag individual run through the Queens Park Rangers' defence in February 1994: "The goal was strange, because at the time it seemed I'd had a pretty straight run to goal – I didn't notice other players. It was only when I saw the replay on the telly after the match that I realised how many players I'd taken on!" When he can make the game look so easy, people can't understand why Giggsy doesn't produce that form all the time.

Although Ryan has been a major player in United's recent years of glory, he hasn't dominated European football as was widely predicted when he burst on the scene. It may seem harsh to criticise Giggsy – after all, no other 23-year-old has two PFA Young Player Of The Year (1993 and 1994) awards tucked away in their trophy cabinet. It's just that with Ryan's world-class gifts, our expectations are higher and he knows it.

"I'm only a year older than the group of players here who are regarded as the young lads," says Ryan. "But because I've been playing in the first team for so long, everyone assumes I should be at my best all the time."

After his brilliant display in United's 4–0 Champions' League stuffing of Porto in March, manager Alex Ferguson said, "In two years, Ryan will be a truly wonderful player." It is true that these are vital years ahead and Ryan is working hard to make them count. "I haven't peaked yet, and the Boss is driving me on to higher standards", says Ryan. "I know I can improve certain aspects of my game, like my crossing, which can be a bit careless at times. My finishing also lets me down too often. I went through a spell at

31

Christmas last season where I was missing a sitter a game and that's really frustrating. I think if I had put all my chances away last season, I would have been one of the top scorers! My highest in a season is 17 goals in the 1993/94 Double season and I want to get back to that level."

In 1997, Ryan Giggs still has the flair but a little less of the devil-may-care attitude of his younger days. In 1993 he said, "At United, we try a few tricks. If they don't come off, so what?" Nowadays, Ryan tends to save his party-piece skills for when the United are 3– or 4–0 up. "I still love to take people on, but if the pass is the better option, I'll pass it. There aren't too many occasions when you can use fancy tricks, because the games are so tight. If I do try a trick and lose the ball, I tend to drift into the middle of the pitch away from the

> ## "It's a hell of a thought to imagine what a player Ryan will be at his peak. It's a really mouth-watering and exciting prospect."
> ### GEORGE BEST

dugout, because I know the Boss will be yelling at me!"

If he stays clear of injury following his hernia op in summer, Giggs should challenge the likes of Bergkamp and Zola for senior Player of the Year awards this year, but personal ambitions take second place for Ryan.

"Our success has been built on teamwork and team spirit. You look for individual magic within a team effort. Sure, certain players will receive special acclaim from the fans and the media, but we all know here that it is the team that must come first."

The United player who received most acclaim in the Nineties is Eric Cantona. Unlike many people, Ryan is confident that Eric's decision to hang up his boots will not stop United's run of glory. "People used to say that when Eric played badly, United didn't play well, but I never agreed with that. Obviously, he was a very important player for us, but we've got enough good players in our squad to do well without Eric."

Whatever happens in the rest of his career, Ryan has already had some great times. "I'm very lucky," he admits. "In the dressing room, we sometimes chat about what it would be like to be mid-table with nothing to play for at the end of the season. I've never experienced that at United."

He probably never will.

THE FIRST TIME I SAW GIGGSY...

No one forgets the first time they saw Ryan Giggs play, but Alex Ferguson thought he performed like a dog! "Even as 13-year-old, Ryan floated over the ground like a wee cocker spaniel chasing a piece of silver paper in the wind," marvelled the canny Scot.

For Andy Mitten, his first sight of Giggsy was less enjoyable. He had to mark him. "I was playing for my local team Victoria Boys against Deans youth team. Someone warned me before the match to look out for their number 11, Ryan Wilson, as he was known at the time. 'He's fast', he said. 'FAST!' I remember thinking after Ryan had skinned me for the third time in nine minutes. I was substituted at half time!"

Andy now writes about Giggs and co in his fanzine, *United We Stand*.

HAVING A LAUGH

On a pre-season trip in 1994, Giggsy, Ince and Dion Dublin were in a hotel lift. Dion was thanking the lift attendant for her help when Giggsy pulled down poor Dion's trackie bottoms, leaving him apologising to the guests while Incey and Ryan ran off laughing. Dion didn't talk to Ryan for hours.

> ## ❝ His talent is God-given. He w when he's got his bus pass, beca

RYAN'S WONDER CURLER

v Coventry (a)
18 January 1997

Giggsy slide-tackles Telfer on the edge of the box and wins the ball cleanly. He jumps up and shapes to hit it

GIGGS CLONED!

In "Doppelganger", Ryan's latest ad campaign for Reebok, cinema buffs enjoyed watching an animated version of Giggsy battle against his evil double cloned from his own saliva. A frighteningly life-like Peter Schmeichel also appeared in the short film.

RYAN'S SHORTS

1 Fan mail
I still get a lot, especially on Valentine's Day, which is nice. My grandparents deal with all the mail because I simply haven't got the time.

2 Fave magazines
I read a lot of men's magazines like *Esquire*, *FHM*, *GQ* and *Arena*.

3 Childhood heroes
Bryan Robson, Ian Rush and Mark Hughes.

4 Fave designer
Armani

5 Cars
I drive an Aston Martin and a Grand Cherokee jeep.

6 Advice for young players
Of course skill and natural talent help, but you've got to practice and practice if you want to make it. Listen to your coaches and don't assume you know it all, because you don't!

7 Fave players
I loved watching Roberto Baggio in his prime. Now, Ronaldo is a bit special. Here at United, I'm playing with most of them, so I'm not going to say any more because they'll get big-headed.

8 Most memorable goal
My free kick against Blackburn in May 1993, when we celebrated United's first Championship for 26 years.

9 Quickest goal
I scored one in 16 seconds on 18 November 1995 against Southampton at Old Trafford. My friends didn't see it. They were still queuing up outside.

10 Most famous person ever met
That must be Nelson Mandela, who I met on our 1993 tour of South Africa.

11 The best
The 1994 Double team is the best I've played in, but I think this team has the potential to be even better.

ill have wonderful skill even
at sort of ability never deserts you. 99 BRIAN KIDD

with his weaker right foot. Ryan's curling shot is unstoppable and he runs off to celebrate (and escape from Roy!)

33

Premium

The Premiership is now the most exciting league in the world and big respect goes to the skilful foreign players that have come to England and got stuck into the fast and furious style of football. It is a sign of Manchester United's worldwide appeal that three of our eight foreigners – Henning, Schmikes and Erik – had always supported United before they played for us. Here's what the Red imports say about their childhood dreams and the reality of life at Old Trafford...

HENNING

"Although I was a Manchester United fan when I was younger, I wasn't one of those really mad supporters. You see fans today wearing all the shirts and their rooms have Man United all over the place. It was never like that for me. I just used to watch the English league on Norwegian television on a Saturday and argue with my brother – he supported Liverpool!"

JORDI

"Four players were there for me when I had a difficult time in my first season – Eric Cantona, Phil Neville, Ole Gunnar and Raimond. It's good to know there are guys in the team who I can always talk to."

RAIMOND

Schmeichel's understudy, handsome Rai Van Der Gouw, has certainly made a big impression on the female staff at Old Trafford. When the Dutchman was told that they'd nicknamed him Van Der Gorgeous he smiled and said, "Is that what they call me? Well, when you get a nickname like that, you can't complain. It's a big compliment."

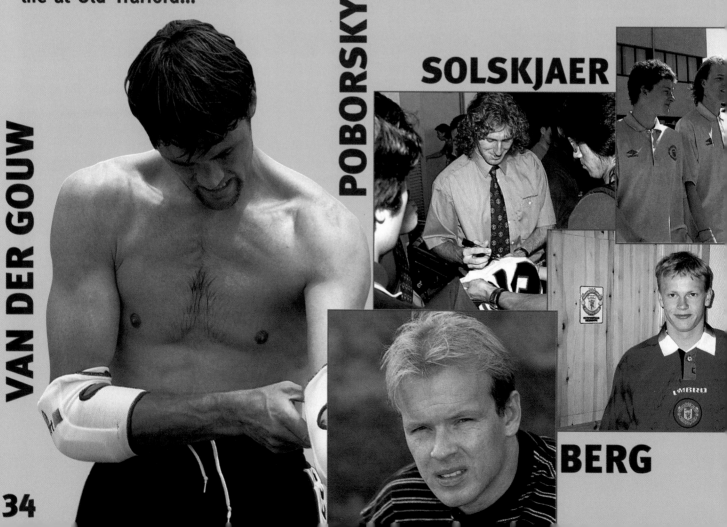

VAN DER GOUW

POBORSKY

SOLSKJAER

BERG

imports

KAREL

"Before I came, as far as I was aware, the English teams didn't have a very good reputation in Europe for their skill. I was quite surprised at how high the standard of football is in this country."

SCHMIKES

"I've always said that if I was ever to move on, it would be to a bigger and better club. But when I look at the size of the club, its stature, the interest around it, United simply *is* the biggest."

ERIK NEV

"I've been a United fan as long as I can remember. My grandfather gave me a United goalie shirt when I was six and I hardly knew the name of any other club. So Gary Bailey became my hero, even though I've never been a goalkeeper. I soon started to listen to the match commentary on the BBC World Service and, when I got older, I travelled to watch United play. I also joined the Scandanavian Supporters Club and bought the Norwegian version of *Manchester United* magazine."

RONNY

"Before I came to Manchester United I spent one year in Besiktas, Turkey and the culture is very different there. It was a fun experience but I couldn't speak the language. I'm very happy to be in England now. Here, you can have a conversation with the player beside you. For Norwegians, England is more suitable than Turkey. Professionally, it is very similar and the lifestyle is similar too."

OLE GUNNAR

I wasn't aware that United were watching me, but when I got the phonecall to say they were interested I was very happy and there was no way I would say no to them. It was a wonderful moment when I signed the contract. I have felt welcomed by the public, the crowd and all the players. I like it here in Manchester very much. Sometimes, I have to pinch myself to see if this is true, that it's really happening."

SCHMEICHEL

CRUYFF

JOHNSEN

NEVLAND

DOUBLE DUTCH
Although Jordi is a Dutch international, he grew up in Spain where his father Johan managed Barcelona.
"I have Dutch blood, but my mentality, my culture and my way of living are definitely Spanish," says Jordi.

SNAP SHOT
Ole Gunnar's girlfriend Silje is a talented photographer. She is currently doing a photography course at Manchester Metropolitan University and some of her photos of Ole Gunnar relaxing in Norway can be seen on the cover of this book.

FORE!
It was Karel's ambition to learn how to play golf in England, but he's finding it hard! "I'm taking lessons from a golf professional at a local course. I've played about 10 rounds in all. I like it but it's really difficult," admits Pob.

HAT-TRICK ERIK
It was unknown striker Erik Nevland's impressive trial in Autumn 1996 that won him a United pro contract. Amazingly, Erik scored two hat-tricks – one for the A team and one for the Reserves – in three games.

FAR OUT, MAN

All professional footballers play pre-season matches to sharpen their fitness for the season ahead. It's just that if you play for a world-famous club like Manchester United, you get to go to nicer places. Our Insider spy went with the players to Thailand, Hong Kong and Japan. This is his behind-the-scenes report on a memorable trip.

Reds mania in Thailand: probably Phil

Welcome to United, Mr Sheringham

ON OUR WAY

When 20 bleary-eyed Manchester United players checked into Manchester airport at 6.15 am on Monday morning, including 15 internationals, three famous names were still tucked up in bed. Giggsy, Becks and Gary Neville were to prepare for the new season with the youth players at the Cliff.

The 14-hour journey to Thailand included a short stop in Paris, but there wasn't time to do much. Teddy, Pally, Nicky and Keano opted for a game of cards while the rest watched TV in the executive lounge. At midday, the players piled on to the plane. Rai Van Der Gouw, having seen the hectic schedule facing the team, put on an eye-mask and grabbed 40 winks. Meanwhile, the wide-awake lads supped soft drinks, put on their headsets and watched the three in-flight movies – the Eddie Murphy film *Metro* and *Earthquake*, starring Tommy Lee Jones, went down particularly well.

Norwegian ham

BANGKOK GOES BONKERS

On touching down in Bangkok, the lads walked into absolute mayhem. The airport was packed tight with over 2,000 Thai Reds desperate to catch a first glimpse of their heroes – and it was 5.30 am! Lots of fans were waving home-made banners. Phil Neville appeared to be the most popular player, but the huge number of flags bearing Michael Clegg and Terry Cooke's names proved that Oriental Reds know all about United stars of the future. It was a brilliant welcome.

A bite of breakfast, an hour's kip, then it was time to train. Whenever and wherever United land in the world, coach Brian Kidd will find a patch of grass so the players can have a loosening up session to get the rust out of their system after the long flight – though, strangely, Kiddo doesn't receive a lot of thanks from the players for his efforts. Four thousand fans attended United's first session at the Thailand national stadium. Solskjaer had a hamstring strain and physio David Fevre put him through some painful stretching exercises, while Kiddo ran the legs off the rest of the squad. Peter Schmeichel, who had come back to pre-season training a week later than the others, was also expecting a hard time. He would have to do extra work in the hotel gym to catch up. At the end of the session, practical joker David May borrowed a microphone from one of the TV newsmen present and conducted his own interview with Gary Pallister, before squirting everyone in sight with water.

> "I got my first impression of how big Man United are out in Bangkok. The number of supporters who followed us around was unbelieveable. I've been there with England and Tottenham and there was a nice turn out, but nothing like that."
>
> **TEDDY SHERINGHAM**

Extra time in the gym for Schmikes and Ole

given a good-luck bracelet made up of seven coloured pieces of string by their Thai hosts.

The next day, Pally, Teddy and Andy Cole went window-shopping in Bangkok. As famous footballers, they expect a bit of protection, but nine bodyguards for three players seemed a bit extreme. The lads hopped into a van with their new muscle-bound friends, who only attracted more attention and, after signing a thousand autographs, the players retired to the Hard Rock Cafe for milkshakes all round.

On matchday, as it was a five o'clock kick-off, there was a morning training session and the players rested before a police

u like toast?

The healing touch of Alex Ferguson

escort guided the team bus to the ground. Teddy Sheringham, on his United debut, shook hands with the brightly dressed Thai team mascot. United ran out comfortable 2–0 winners with a goal from Nicky Butt and an own goal by Thailand's Tongsukkaew.

That night, Fergie allowed the lads a couple of beers at the hotel, and most headed for the amazing top floor bar with stunning views over Bangkok. Even in the hotel, the ever-present bodyguards were keeping supporters away from the players, but United fans don't give up easily – Brian McClair signed one autograph in the gents toilets.

e love

In the evening, the players went to the the offices of a large Bangkok newspaper for a welcome party. Each of the players got on the microphone to introduce themselves to the guests, then a huge line of people formed a queue to offer gifts to Alex Ferguson. Later the players were treated to displays of traditional Thai dancing and boxing (the younger players thought one of the boxers was the spitting image of Tommy Smith, an ex-United youth player). When the players left the party, each was

When Teddy, Andy and Pally visited the Hard Rock Café in Thailand, the manager showed the boys photos of Robbie Fowler who had been there with his mates last summer.

WELL RED

English versions of the club's official magazines (Manchester United and Glory Glory Man United) sell over 20,000 copies per month in the Far East. The mags are also translated into other languages. Thai versions of Manchester United sell 20,000 copies in Thailand, while 10,000 Cantonese people in Hong Kong follow the Reds progress through the magazine too. The mag has just been launched in China as well.

Match programmes from Bangkok, Hong Kong and Tokyo

United are big news wherever they go

HONG KONG HOORAY

Landing an aeroplane in Hong Kong is a pretty dodgy business and the players were gasping as their plane weaved its way between the city skyscrapers. The welcome at the airport was a just as enthusiastic (if less chaotic) than in Bangkok. At the plush Grand Hyatt Hotel Teddy, who stayed there with England last year, showed the lads around. The team's rooms were all on the 16th floor, but the tennis courts on the 11th floor were the place to be during the stay.

Here comes group Z

Ben Thornley proved to be the best player in doubles matches with Cleggy, Phil Mulryne and Terry Cooke. On the second day, veterans McClair and Irwin challenged Clegg and Mulryne to a battle of ages. The old guys won, much to Denis's surprise. "I haven't played since I was at school," he gasped.

Chairman Martin Edwards also invited members of the Hong Kong Branch of the United Supporters' Club into the hotel for a drink and a chat with the players and staff. Like everything in Hong Kong, it was very well organised. Before training, the players did a big autograph session at the Hong Kong stadium. Fans came in one group at a time, and as groups A, B, C, D and E all passed through, Teddy and Choccy were getting writer's cramp. They asked our Insider Guide photographer how many more groups were left. "Well, I've just seen someone wearing a 'Z' badge," he chuckled.

After a good training session in warm rain, it was back to the hotel for dinner. Even on tour, the players have to keep to a healthy

Refuelling at the Grand Hyatt hotel

Fancy trying to land a plane in Hong Kong?

For the kids, honest

> "We got a brilliant reception in Thailand, Hong Kong and Japan. We feel very privileged to have supporters all over the world. It's tiring to travel half way round the globe to play, but it's only fair because the people are so fanatical."
> **ROY KEANE**

diet. Although they were staying at a five-star hotel, there was no chance of puddings from the sweet trolley. Top athletes need plenty of carbohydrates and not too much fat if they are to keep running for 90 minutes. United's resident dietitian Trevor Lea always phones hotels in advance and tells them what food he wants on the menu. Brian McClair calls it 'fuel', not food, and says it's a bonus if he likes it. Fortunately, the food in Hong Kong was good. The Chicken Satay and Chicken Tikka dishes were voted the players' favourites of the tour.

After dinner it was time for a late-night shopping trip. Keano bought some toys for his kids, Kiddo bought himself a new camera and Coley and Scholesy checked out the latest mini video-cameras.

On matchday, a few fans who had travelled all the way from Manchester were spotted in a 36,000 crowd which did it's own Oriental version of the Mexican wave. United beat South China 1–0 with Jordi Cruyff heading a late winner. Roy Keane picked up his first trophy as United captain.

After the game, Ferguson told the players to go out and enjoy themselves, but like Cinderella, they were all tucked up in bed before midnight.

An Oriental wave

I wonder what "Ejector seat" does?

On the morning of the game, there was nowhere for the players to train. Kiddo wasn't pleased but a few tired players were relieved. In the dressing room pre-match, a photo of Brian Kidd in his playing days was pinned up on the wall. One of the players had cut it out of the match programme and the lads were in fits of laughter when they saw Kiddo in his prime.

United played Urawa Red Diamonds in their last match of the tour. The Japanese J–League team has been modelled on

Brian Kidd in his prime, from the match programme, raised a laugh in the dressing room before the Urawa Red Diamonds game

You shouldn't have

Sniff, sniff... yeuch

It helps me catch the ball on my knees

I'm sure no one will miss just one can

Not good in the mornings

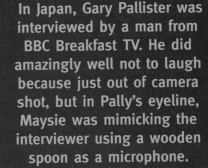

In Japan, Gary Pallister was interviewed by a man from BBC Breakfast TV. He did amazingly well not to laugh because just out of camera shot, but in Pally's eyeline, Maysie was mimicking the interviewer using a wooden spoon as a microphone.

BIG IN JAPAN

The next day, an early flight from Hong Kong transferred the team to Tokyo. A couple of hundred fans turned up at Narita airport to greet the players. The traffic in Tokyo is pretty horrendous. There were a few moans and groans from the players, tired out by the heat and all the travelling, during the two-and-a-half hour crawl to the hotel.

When the players reached their hotel rooms, the hi-tech bathrooms caused a stir. According to Brian McClair, his had "an all-singing, all-dancing toilet seat that heated up, dried, made toast and coffee and there was a mini TV to watch while you shaved too".

Manchester United and wear the famous red, white and black colours too. They didn't play like United though. Ole Gunnar's two goals were enough to secure a 2–1 win and another trophy for captain Keane.

In Hong Kong, coach Brian Kidd bought himself a nice new camera, but he needn't have bothered. A Japanese fan was so pleased that United came to visit, he gave Kiddo an even better camera worth £250!

HOME SWEET HOME

The players had a great time in the Far East, but all the travelling and jet lag finally caught up with them. Most slept their way through the flight home, but the Boss could be seen crying with laughter at the in-flight comedy movie. Back at Manchester Airport the players' wives and girlfriends were there to greet them. Everyone headed home except for one poor player who couldn't find his luggage at baggage claim. After a while, he realised someone has already taken it off the conveyer belt. David May is never too tired to play a practical joke.

39

MODI

DAVID BECKHAM has got the talent, he's got the looks and he's certainly got goal power. In summer 1996, after helping Gary and Phil, Scholesy and Butty prove that you can win the Double with kids, Becks did his first-ever photo session at a secret location in Manchester. Boss Alex Ferguson, keen to protect his rising star from too much exposure, wouldn't allow the pictures to be seen until Becks was more established. Now, for the first time ever, here are a selection of shots from the premier shoot with Britain's hottest football property. The hair may be longer now, but there's no mistaking that cheeky cockney grin and Becks' Brylcreem-boyish looks...

▲ "You looking at me."

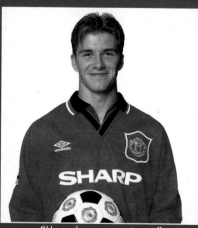

"How do you want me."

"Who says I've got football on the brain."

▼ "Now, that's what you call a quiff."

▲ "Quick, hide! Keano's coming round the corner."

CITIZEN

"The boy-next-▶ door? Me? Never."

"No more photos, lads. ▶ I'm cream-crackered – Kiddo had us running for two hours solid this morning."

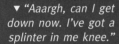

▼ "Aaargh, can I get down now. I've got a splinter in me knee."

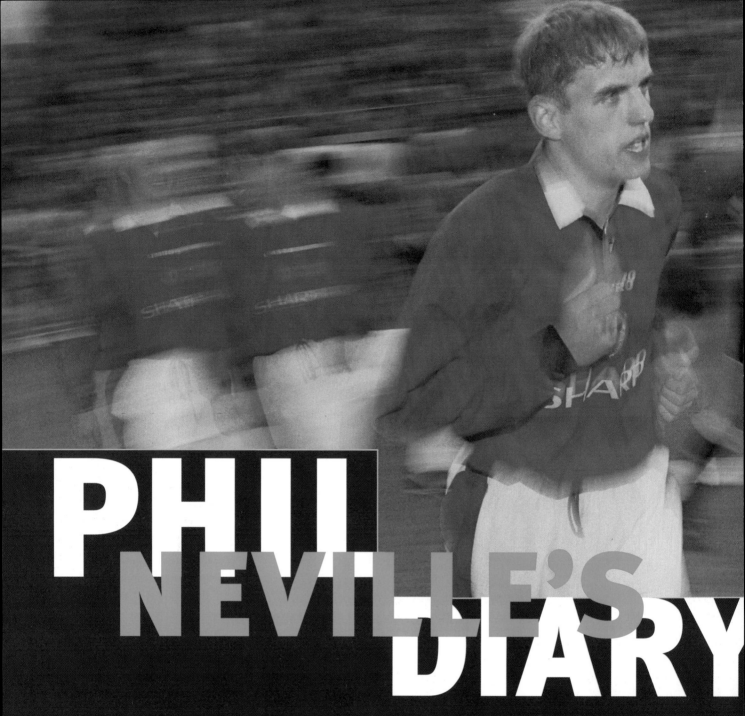

PHIL NEVILLE'S DIARY

What's it really like to play for Manchester United? In August, Phil Neville kept a day-by-day diary to show you exactly how it is...

Friday 22 August

Training this morning. It's just a light 45-minute session as we have a game tomorrow. We play 7-a-side; youngsters against the old ones. I have Becks, Butt, Scholesy, Gary, Terry Cooke and Phil Mulryne on my side and we play against the 'Olds': Denis Irwin, Roy Keane and the rest. We score first, but then we get absolutely hammered 5–1. We play against benches outside so there is only a small target to hit. The olds have Rai Van Der Gouw on their side who just stands there and blocks everything, whereas we have Becks trying to protect the target, who isn't the greatest! It is very competitive. We really want to beat the old ones and tackles fly in from Butty and Giggsy. Whenever it gets too rough the manager stops it, but it's just a bit of a laugh before the match on Saturday.

This is only Hening Berg's second day in training. I am really impressed with him; he looks very cool, like he never breaks into a sweat. First-class player and trainer. I gather he is a big United fan as well. It doesn't suprise me as United are very popular with Norwegians. A few times a year I meet groups of Norwegian fans when they come over to Manchester.

22.08.97

Rai blocks everything

Gary wakes up early and get the papers at about seven, reads them and then goes back to sleep. He wakes me up rustling about and then goes back to sleep himself, after telling me I can't read the papers!

The team doesn't normally have breakfast together. Brian McClair, Peter Schmeichel and Giggsy go down for breakfast, but my brother and I have it in our room.

We have a pre-match meal at 12 and then at 12:45 we have a team meeting about the game where the manager discusses tactics. He doesn't announce the team, but he tells those who played in the last game if they won't be playing, so he pulls me and Scholesy aside and tells us that we are on the bench for this one. It is just a case of Gary needing a game and I am the unlucky one. I am a bit disappointed as I've played all the games up until now, but if I am honest, I expected it as he is never going to leave out Denis Irwin. The meeting lasts 25 minutes and it consists of the manager standing at the front of the room in front of a tactics board and going through the formation of the team.

We leave the hotel at 1.15 and it is only a 20-minute drive to Filbert Street. It is quite good at Leicester as the fans are cordoned off so you can get in and out without any

hassle. We arrive at the ground early so some of the lads take the chance to have a chat with Leicester's new signing Rob Savage who was with all of us at Manchester United as a youth player.

We all get changed and go out to warm up. During shooting practice in the warm-ups, Becks accidentally hits a nine-year-old Leicester fan in the face with a shot. He goes straight up to him, apologises and tells him to come and see him after the game when Becks gives him his boots. They are an expensive pair, so it is a tremendous gesture by Becks. He does a lot of things like that, giving boots to disabled fans, but it goes unseen.

I'm a very agitated watcher of games when I'm on the bench. I'm very lively and jump out of my seat when I think we have scored, so people next to me get annoyed and say, "Sit down, Phil, sit down!" I run along the sidelines to get rid of the nervous energy. We get some terrible abuse from the Leicester fans, some is good banter, but some is a bit nasty.

We have the better chances, but before the game we knew it was going to be difficult as they had just beaten Liverpool at Anfield, so we are reasonably pleased with a point. We're not going to hit the post three times in a game and not score very many times. Giggsy has a great game, at times he is unbelievable. Teddy doesn't say much, so you don't know what he is thinking, but he is probably disappointed at his miss, but everyone misses chances.

We leave the ground at 5.45 and as soon as I get on the coach I find out the cricket score from the Sixth Test at the Oval between England and Australia. The Aussies are 100-9. I can't believe it. When I last heard, England were still batting. I am just in time to see Tuffnell take the last wicket and everyone is really happy. During the series, I had the Australian captain Mark

The manager handles all the Press. He likes to do all the talking and let us just concentrate on preparing for the game. It is the summer holidays, so there are loads of fans and autograph-hunters down at the Cliff. It is a bit difficult as I have to rush off to get ready for tomorrow's game at Leicester, so I can't sign everything.

I go home quickly, pack my bag, have a bite to eat and then travel to the coach pick-up point for lads who live on the North side of Manchester where I meet Scholesy, Kiddo, Giggsy, Terry Cooke and Henning Berg.

The journey to Leicester is two and a half hours. There is a speed limit on coaches of 62 mph, so all the lads have a moan and call it the "Milk Float". It is really hot as well. The coach is split into two halves; down the front is me, Nicky, and Giggsy on one floor and then on the other floor is David Beckham and Jimmy Curran – who does the massages before the games – and Albert the kitman. The manager, Pally, Keano and Denis Irwin play cards at the back. We watch *Four Weddings and a Funeral* which we've seen 10 times before and Gary bought the new Oasis CD, which we listen to. It is obvious to other motorists who we are as there is a massive Red Devil on the side of the coach, so they slow down and have a look. We pass them about four times, because they like to wave to us.

We can't get into the Leicester hotel that we stayed in last season so we stay in a new one. We're a bit disappointed that they don't have *Sky* as we want to watch the Man City game. We have dinner at seven, when we are asked if we need any Vitamin C, and then the rest of the evening we are free to do what we want. There are no team talks, the manager keeps himself to himself when we get to the hotel. We don't see him until the next morning.

I room with my brother, Gary. Some lads stay up late, but Gary and me usually like to get to bed early. We are in bed by about 10 and we are asleep by 10.30. There is no lights out or curfew, it's just a trust thing.

Spag bol pre-match

Hanging loose in the hotel lobby

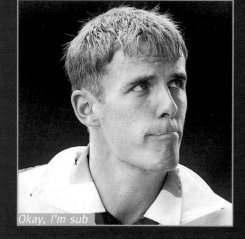

Okay, I'm sub

A slurp and a smile

Saturday, and with a game on Wednesday, training is very competitive with all the lads looking to impress. Because we have three games in a week, we don't do too much and we are actually only in for an hour. But it is an enjoyable session, everyone gets a sweat on. The lads give Teddy a bit of stick for his miss on Saturday and he just smiles, but it is nothing serious as we all know he is under enough pressure as it is.

There is an emphasis on shooting this morning, the manager wants us to sharpen it up and get more shots in on goal. I don't score, I just get in the way and get hit a lot! I haven't scored for the first team yet, but I'm hoping I'll get one this season, especially since Gary scored his first one last year against Middlesbrough and he has a pop at me that I haven't managed one yet. In fact on Saturday he was having a laugh because his odds on scoring were a lot shorter than mine. Gary was 40–1 and I was

Taylor's wife and kids staying at my house, because my family have been friends with him since he played for my team Greenmount before he broke in to the Australian team. Mark wanted to give his family a base as it wouldn't have been nice to constantly move his kids around the country to different hotels. We went out for a couple of meals during the summer.

My dad picks Gary and I up at the drop-off point at 8.30 pm and then I see my girlfriend and watch Match of the Day.

Sunday 24 August

I enjoy a lay-in this morning as we have no training. I look at the papers which contain the news of England's thrilling test win. Sometimes I think what could have been if I had chosen cricket as my career, but I know I made the right decision in choosing football. It is so much more exciting playing in front of 55,000 at Old Trafford rather than just a few thousand on the county circuit. I haven't really had a chance to pick up a bat for a couple of years now, as the last two summers I have been involved with Euro '96 and then Le Tournoi.

I go out to lunch with my parents and then we go to see Gary's house which is in the process of being built. It is a barn which he is converting. It's going slowly, but it's going well. I have a game of snooker when I get home. I just take it easy this evening as I've got training tomorrow and a busy week ahead. I hope I'll get back in the team this week. I'm sure the manager will look to get me a game before the England squad is picked. Glenn Hoddle announces the squad on Friday and I hope to be in it.

Monday 25 August

No Bank Holiday for me, so I get into training about 10 am. There is a feeling of disappointment around because of Saturday; all the lads felt we should have won. Because of our failure to win on

Shooting practice: one day I'll actually score

something like 60–1! I haven't been that close to scoring, but I did hit the post on my debut against Wrexham over two years ago.

I have a chat with Jordi Cruyff. He is really disappointed with getting injured. He blames himself because it was his poor touch that allowed the ball to run away and then he got injured trying to retrieve it. I'm quite close to Jordi, I've been around to his house and we really get on. I helped him last season when he was really down. I would give him encouragement and tell him to give it all a chance. He has done well in pre-season and in the games so far. Before I leave training I sign about 100 autographs. There are about five or six of us going down the line signing things. There seems to be more of them every day.

In the evening I go to see my mate David Gardner play for Witton Albion against Congleton. David helps them to a 5–1 win. He was at United with me as an apprentice,

Don't we look stylish?

but they let him go and he had some time at Man City but they let him go as well. He's been searching for a new team for a while. Macclesfield took him and loaned him out to Witton to build himself up.

I get home and ask my dad the Blackburn score and he says '7–2'. I tell him to give over, but he is right. Roy Hodgson is going to do a great job for them.

Tuesday 26 August

The manager announces the team for the game against Everton tomorrow and, unfortunately, I'll be on the bench again. At the same meeting the manager speaks about tactics; how he expects Everton to play and how he wants us to play. We then play a practice match for about 15 minutes with the team for Wednesday playing against the other lads who pretend to be Everton. I am at left back, so I must be Terry Phelan.

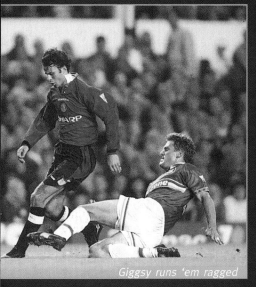
Giggsy runs 'em ragged

We don't play at full pace and there are no tackles put in as we want to avoid injuries. It is really just shadow play. We then spend 10 minutes on set pieces as well.

Usually, we then do some shooting to give the goalkeepers some handling practice, but today we have a photo session for the new Champions' League kit, which looks really nice. It is a brighter red than the home kit, with white socks which we prefer. We pose for a team shot and then individual shots. It only takes 10 minutes.

I have lunch with Jordi where we discuss tomorrow's game and also the Champions' League draw. He hopes we get drawn with Barcelona as he would love to go back there and he thinks he would get a good reception from the fans.

In the evening I go to see Bury versus Crewe in the Coca-Cola Cup with my dad. My mum and dad both work for Bury so they have always been my second team and I try to see as many of their home games as possible. We aren't treated like superstars who play for Man United, just like normal lads as we have been going there for years.

Wednesday 27 August

I meet up with the other lads at Old Trafford where we get the coach down to Liverpool. It is only a 25-minute journey to the hotel. We have some lunch and then retire to our rooms for a sleep. Gary and I sleep for about three and a half hours until

> **"David Beckham is in *The Sun* today as he has been voted the best-looking man in the world... we have a laugh at Giggsy who is way behind in 34th place or something"**

4.30 pm. I always sleep in the afternoons before a game. It doesn't make me feel groggy at all. I am substitute so I have to be quiet to let my brother sleep.

Before we leave the hotel, we have a snack and then the manager gives a team talk. The team was named yesterday, so it is just to go over tactics. Ronny Johnsen pulls out through injury so Henning keeps his place. Giggsy's new role in the side is discussed. He is going to play centre forward with Teddy and Scholesy behind him. Ryan gives us some more pace up front and playing in this position has worked before

against Everton.

We set off from the hotel at about 6.15 pm with a police escort. I think it's Premier League rules to have one now. Its not so we can go through red lights, but just in case anything happens. Some people spit and throw things at the coach and give us two fingers, but nothing serious has happened yet. Sometimes we'll leave an away ground and stop at some lights by a pub with 20 opposition supporters standing outside and they'll gesture and throw things. It happened at Tottenham for the opening game of the season but, fortunately, we have shatter-proof glass on our coaches! They are not fitted on foreign coaches, so last year in Turkey we got showered in glass when someone threw a stone.

David Beckham is in the *Sun* today as he has been voted the best-looking man in the world. Some of the players give him some stick, saying that he has gone out and bought every copy of the *Sun* in England. He protests that he hadn't seen it. Knowing Becks, I believe it, as he doesn't pay much attention to the papers these days. We have a laugh at Giggsy who is way behind in 34th place or something.

Becks is getting more and more attention and I think he is handling it really well. I think it has improved his performances on the field and he is working harder. He is so much under the microscope that he has to play well in every game.

The sort of pressure both Becks and Giggsy are under doesn't look nice at all. I don't think you appreciate how hard it is until you have sampled it yourself and, to be honest, I wouldn't want to at all. I'm more than happy with things as they are.

I am on the bench again. Andy Cole gets on, but coming back from injury he needs a run out. Tonight is the best performance of the season so far. Giggsy is world class and everyone is happy for Teddy to get his first goal

A quiet corner at the Cliff

That is four games played and no goals conceded now, at this stage last year we had already let in about five. Before the season started, the manager questioned our defending last season and said we had to improve and I think we have done that. Steve Bruce's departure and not having a settled defence didn't help us, but the defence seems to have a better understanding of each other now and it shows by keeping four clean sheets.

Thursday 28 August

The players that didn't play last night train with the Reserves this morning and the other lads just have a light session. There are 24 of us so it is a bit hectic. We are in three teams of eight and we play one game on, one game off. Then we do a little bit of running. Ronny is still suffering a bit with his injury and won't be fit for Saturday's game.

Everyone is talking about the European draw tomorrow. I sit next to Jordi and Ole Gunnar at dinner. Ole's not progressing as quickly as he hoped with his injury. It's his first injury of this type and he is pretty wary about pushing it. He should be back before the first European game. We have a chat about the Leicester game. I haven't seen Dennis Bergkamp's hat-trick yet but I heard it was brilliant. Jordi is good friends with Dennis and is really pleased for him. I rest all afternoon as I am tired from yesterday's trip. I go to my Gran's for tea and then go to see my girlfriend for an hour.

Friday 29 August

We do a long warm-up this morning as a few of the lads are still stiff from Wednesday because the pitch was really hard. There are loads of photographers and cameramen down at the Cliff because of the European draw. They are allowed to film training so the lads have to watch their language a bit! We play youngsters against olds again. The olds moan that they don't want to play as they always beat us, so it is good to beat them 4–3. Giggsy is the oldest of the youngsters and he says he will never play for the olds, no matter how old he gets! Rai plays in goal for us today. He is actually older than Peter, but Peter says he would never go in goal for us!

We finish before noon and I stay behind for some treatment for a knock I got in training. The Boss won't announce the team until tomorrow at 1.30 pm. If we are playing at home, he usually doesn't tell us who is in the team until the day of the match. Afterwards I pose for a few photos

because I am taking charge of the letters page in *Glory Glory Man United* magazine.

Gary rings me later on the mobile to tell me who we have drawn in the European Cup. I think he's more interested in what the food is going to be like in the hotels! The food we had in Volgograd was not too clever – it was probably the worst hotel we've ever stayed in – and in Poland, with England, it was pretty grim too.

> **"Gary rings me on the mobile to say who we've drawn in the European Cup. I think he's more interested in what the food is going to be like in the hotels! The food we had in Volgograd was not too clever – it was probably the worst hotel we've ever stayed in – and in Poland, with England, it was pretty grim too."**

We are all quite happy with the draw. Kiddo thought we would end up with Juventus and hopefully our experience of playing them last year will help. I don't know much about Feyenoord but Dutch teams always play good football. We like playing at Rotterdam and have obviously got fond memories of the stadium with the Cup Winners' Cup win there in '91. It's going to be tough this year with more groups and lots of quality teams. The team who eventually wins it will deserve it after getting through all the group games.

Gary and I have to attend a question and answer session with the Larne supporters association who are over from Northern Ireland. We have a buffet, sign some autographs and answer some questions from some of the younger supporters. We all have a bit of a laugh when someone asks Gary if he is worried about Henning Berg's arrival. I don't think Gary has anything to worry about, though.

My dad phones my mum to find out about the England squad and then gives us both a thumbs up from the back of the room to let us now we are in. There are a few new faces: Rio Ferdinand, Emile Heskey and Stuart Ripley. It's also good to see Pally back in the squad. He's one of the best cen-

Guess who's the new letters editor?

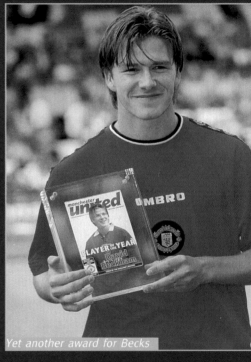
Yet another award for Becks

tre halves in England and, with the current injuries, he is likely to play. It would be great to be picked for the starting line-up. I played in all three games in Le Tournoi, so hopefully I stand a good chance.

I go to see my girlfriend and then my brother's barn. I then head home and spend the rest of the evening relaxing and watching a bit of TV. Players are not allowed out to go drinking or to go to nightclubs on a Friday night, so we keep a low profile.

Saturday 30 August

I get up quite early and read the papers. I call in at the Cliff on my way to Old Trafford to pick up my boots for England next week.

I watch a bit of the A team's game.

I arrive at 12 pm at Old Trafford. We have a light pre-match meal of things like toast, beans, spaghetti and scrambled eggs. Then we go and relax in the players' lounge, where no friends or family are allowed in before the game.

The players have a rota where we go and do presentations up in the VIP suites and it is my turn today. Everyone has to do three or four each season.

At about 1.30 pm Kiddo comes in and says that the manager wants a meeting. We all file into the dressing room and sit around as the manager stands in front of a tactician board. He names the team and it is nice to hear my name read out. He told me earlier in the week that I might be playing, but it is nice to be included and hear the back four read out as 'Neville, Pallister, Berg and Neville'. The team talk lasts about 20 minutes and then the manager says, "All

the best, lads." That is the last we see of him until about 2.50 pm.

We watch *Grandstand* and old United videos. Peter likes to go in the warm-up room, I have a kick about and do some stretches. We go out for a warm up at about 2.30 pm. The ground is quite empty at the time. At about 2.50 pm, Kiddo goes in and that is the signal to follow. Becks stays out for a couple of Player of the Year presentations. There isn't any team talk at this point, every one shakes each other's hand and wishes them all the best. Peter is always the first by the door, Keaney's the last, then we walk out. I'm usually third in the line that walks out. I get a few nerves before a game, especially in the tunnel but I think that is a good thing.

It is a warm day and the pitch is quite dry, which might explain our lethargic performance. I haven't played for two and a half weeks so I think I am quite average. We scored really early against Coventry last year, so it is *deja vu* when Coley scores after only a minute. I have to mark Darren Huckerby. He's very fast but I think I do well against him. I get taken off in the second half because I have a bang on my head. I went for a header with Paul Telfer and his elbow accidently hit my head.

The final score of 3–0 flatters us a bit. Afterwards in the dressing room, the manager tells us he's pleased with the win, but not with the performance. He says we shouldn't be complacent and that we need to raise our game against teams like Coventry, which is sometimes harder to do than against the bigger teams. We then watch the telly to find out the other results and some drinks and sandwiches are brought in. I then shower and go into the lounge to meet up with my mum, dad, sister and girlfriend. I leave the ground at 5.45 pm and, while security are getting my car, I sign some autographs.

Gary and I go out with our girlfriends and parents for a meal. I am really tired and have a headache from the bang on my head. So we go home and watch *Match of the Day*. Then I'm woken by my brother at about 1.30 am who tells me that Diana, Princess of Wales is badly injured in a car crash and that Dodi has been killed. Then I fall back to sleep. In the morning everybody is up watching TV and my mum tells me Diana has died. I am completely shocked. There is a sombre mood in the house, my Dad sits in front of the TV all day.

The whole thing puts football into perspective. You have fans baying for your blood and then something like this happens. It just shows how unimportant football is.

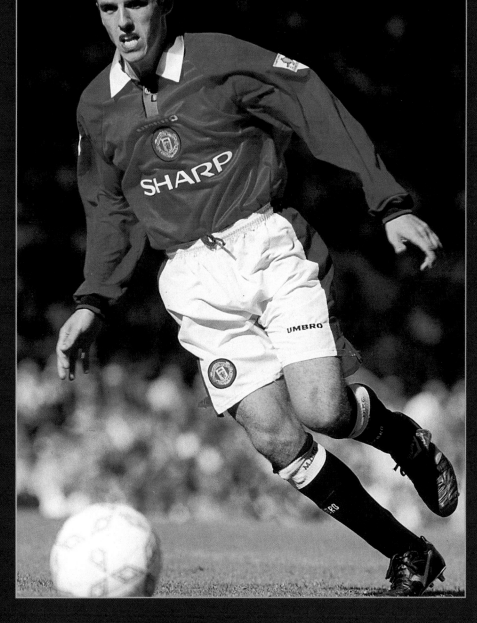

Back in action against Coventry

SHER

"I couldn't be happier than I am now... I'm playing for the best club in the world"

DAVID BECKHAM

When Teddy Sheringham heard the news that Eric Cantona had retired, his first thought was that this could be his chance to join Manchester United. Fortunately for him, Alex Ferguson had similiar thoughts. Just a month later, the deal was done.

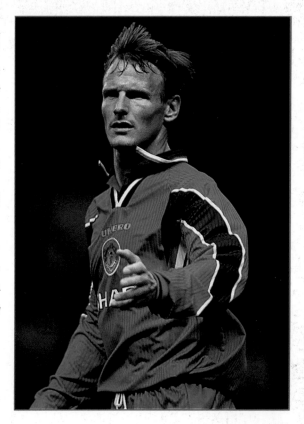

TEDDY
INGHAM

" **I** was very excited when I first heard Manchester United were interested in me. I couldn't wait to get up there, and there was no way I was going to leave without signing."

Life at Tottenham had become frustrating for Teddy. He wanted to win trophies, but he didn't think he could achieve that at White Hart Lane. "I felt that I had given Tottenham the chance to show me their ambition was as big as mine," he says. "I waited and waited, but I was getting older and I could not wait any longer."

Before coming to United, Teddy had only one significant honour to show from his 12 year career, a Second Division Championship medal from his time at Millwall. "It's not exactly a bare cupboard at home, but it's not the biggest collection and I want to make up for that. I won the Golden Boot as top Premiership goalscorer in 1993, but that's something that in a few years' time someone might see in my house and say, 'I forgot you won that.' It's

not something people remember in your club's history. Something lasting."

Teddy didn't have to wait long for his first medal as a United player. He picked up one at the Charity Shield against Chelsea. "It was nice to get my first trophy within a few weeks of joining the club."

Teddy began his career at Millwall in 1985. He would go on to become the club's all-time leading goalscorer, but only after a difficult start. He was loaned out to the Swedish side Djurgardens IF and to Third Division Aldershot, where his main memories are of "being battered by a massive centre half, knocked to the floor by crunching tackles from behind on a cold Tuesday night, and thinking 'I don't need this!'"

After 244 appearances and 111 goals over six years at Millwall, Teddy left for Nottingham Forest in 1991. He spent only one season there, under Brian Clough, who would later regret selling the striker he liked to call 'Edward'. In the summer of 1992, Teddy

moved to Tottenham, "the one club I had always wanted to play for". It was in his very first season at White Hart Lane that Teddy was the Premiership's top scorer with 21 goals.

As a boy Teddy was a Tottenham fan, and his hero was the current England manager Glenn Hoddle. Teddy would turn up early to games at White Hart Lane just to watch Hoddle warm up. "I loved to watch him even in the warm-ups, with his tricks and his turns," he remembers.

"The only reason I first went to see Tottenham play was because of Glenn Hoddle. He was absolutely magnificent, his first touch, his vision, his awareness... just brilliant. I loved Spurs from then on."

During his five years at Tottenham, Teddy developed a reputation as one of England's finest strikers. His most enjoyable time there was the season he spent alongside Jurgen Klinsmann. "He was a World Cup winner and there was an aura about him when he walked on to the pitch. Other players respect him. That rubbed off on me, it was a great experience to play with him." With Klinsmann, Dumitrescu, Anderton and Barmby, he formed Tottenham's Famous Five. "Up front we were dynamite and very entertaining, but we're in this to win things and we never would have. We needed more work on the defence." And Klinsmann was full of praise for his former team mate: "Teddy is the best strike partner I've ever had," he said. "We could play blind together. Instinctively we knew where to find each other."

Alex Ferguson was always an open admirer of Teddy. In his 1995 diary *A Year in the Life*, Ferguson called him "the best link player in England", so in the light of Eric Cantona's retirement he contacted Tottenham first for a replacement. He thought £6 million was too much for a 31 year old, but when the price was lowered to £3.5 million Teddy was signed within 24 hours.

Among his English contemporaries, Teddy's style of play is unique. It worked brilliantly at Euro '96 where he fed Alan Shearer and scored twice himself. "Dropping deep is the natural way I play," he says. "I look for space as the penalty area isn't always the place to be. That's how I've always played my football. It's not a conscious thing that I drop back, but its how I enjoy the game and, luckily, managers seem to like it too.

"I can only play the way I know how, and it's very hard to do anything else. You couldn't ask me to do Ian Wright's job and he probably couldn't do mine. I like to drop back, see what's going on. If it helps the team, I'm happy to drop back into midfield, even defence. I'm not an out-and-out striker and I'm not a defender, but I like to combine the lot."

MY GREATEST GAME

Euro '96
v Holland (h), 4–1
"That was what dreams were made of.
The games for England before Euro '96 against Switzerland, Bulgaria and Croatia showed what I could do. My performance against the Dutch in the tournament was the icing on the cake."

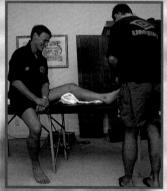

" I do en

sam

"I was very flash when I was young, I thought knew everything. George Graham brought me down to earth with a bump at Millwall. "

TEDDY'S TOP TEN

1 **First pair of football boots?**
A pair of fake Adidas. They had orange stripes and I thought they were great, but I got loads of stick at school

2 **First ever car?**
A blue Vauxhall Viva – it cost me £200

3 **Fave designer?**
The late Versace, but not the really wild stuff

4 **Fave music?**
Rod Stewart

5 **Fave TV programme?**
Friends

6 **Fave food?**
McDonalds. When you have to eat healthily all the time, it's nice to be able to eat junk food now and again

7 **Last CD bought?**
A compilation disc for my journeys from Manchester to London

8 **Fave striker ever?**
Kenny Dalglish

9 **Best advice for a young footballer?**
Firstly to believe in yourself and keep trying. I was always told I was too slow everywhere I went but I just kept on going!

10 **Biggest influence on your career?**
My Dad

TEDDY TIPS

LONG-RANGE PASSES

"This is an important part of my game. It's always been a part of how I play. If you practice, then the confidence to try these long passes will come. The way to do it is to be upfield and then sprint back to the centre circle, find space and look for a midfielder's run before hitting a long-range pass."

THE SHUFFLE

"My dad always taught me to do this as a kid. If you pretend to shoot or cross and you don't, then it will buy you some more time and space to decide what to do with the ball. The best way to do it is when you get the ball to look up or drop your shoulder, as if you plan to do something, then move the ball in the opposite direction."

FAR POST HEADER

"You go to the near post and try to find space. When the corner is flighted over, you run to the far post to lose your defender and head the ball goalwards. It worked best for me against the Dutch in Euro '96."

aining, but I love having a moan at the me, which is all part of being a footballer e. I go on runs, have a moan, and feel great. "

Phil and Gary Neville, Paul Scholes, Nicky Butt and David Beckham all seemed to come from nowhere to make it big. But they had to work their way through Manchester United's tough youth system to get to the top. Fergie knew his fledglings had the ability, but did they have the attitude to handle life at Britain's biggest club? The answer was yes...

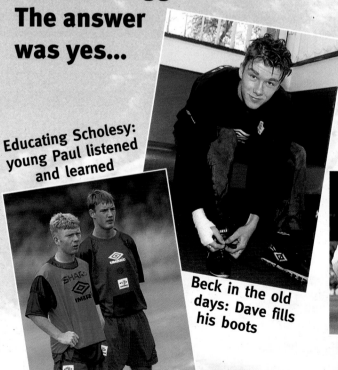

Educating Scholesy: young Paul listened and learned

Beck in the old days: Dave fills his boots

Suited for success: Butty wins the 1994 Reserve Player of the Year award

Born to win: Cap'n Gary lifts the Lancashire League trophy in 1994

Born to win 2: Cap'n Phil lifts the Lancashire FA Youth Cup in 1994

Mixing with the big boys: Becks' first tour with the first team, to South Africa, 1993

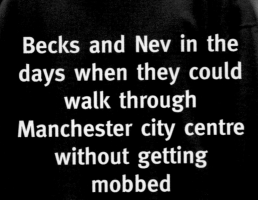

Becks and Nev in the days when they could walk through Manchester city centre without getting mobbed

Phil Neville and Terry Cooke learn the sweeper system the hard way

Rare bird: Gary Nev flies through the air to score for the youth team

Care in the community: Scholesy and Becks bring cheer on a Christmas visit to a local hospital

Free-kick specialist: practice made perfect for Becks

53

When Roy joined Manchester United in the summer of 1993, he became English football's most expensive footballer. Some critics felt the £3.75 million price tag was a tad expensive, but his new team-mate Paul Ince had no doubts. "In a couple of years he'll be worth double", said the Guv'nor. He was wrong. Double double winner Keane is now priceless...

ROY KEANE

"I wouldn't swap him for anyone," said Alex Ferguson when Roy signed the contract that will keep him at Old Trafford until the year 2000. "His peak years are ahead of him – and the ones that have just gone haven't been too bad!" Fergie knows that Roy's competitiveness in midfield makes him the most feared opponent in the Premiership. It's hard to believe that seven years ago, Manchester United's highest-paid player was playing part-time football in Ireland for just £25 a game, wondering if an English League club would ever give him a chance.

"There always seemed to be someone after me but nothing seemed to happen," remembers Roy. Finally, in 1990, Nottingham Forest moved for him. "I played for a team called Rockmount in

Cork from the age of nine to 17. Brilliant years. Then after eight months at Cobh Ramblers, I transferred to Nottingham Forest. I got spotted playing a youth team match for Cobh Ramblers, where we actually lost 4–0! Anyway, afterwards the Chairman came up to me and said there was a scout from Forest who had shown some interest in me. I thought to myself, 'I've heard that one before.' Well, a week later I got a phone call from Forest and that was it."

At Forest, it didn't take Roy long to impress their eccentric manager Brian Clough. "Roy is a charming young man," gushed Cloughie, who gave young Keane his first-team debut against Liverpool less than three weeks after his 19th birthday. "I only had to watch him for 20 minutes in the Reserves to decide that he was a first team player."

55

Cloughie wasn't so pleased about Roy's over-the-top goal celebrations, though. After scoring the winning goal in an FA Cup tie for Forest, delighted Roy did a somersault. Deadpan Clough said afterwards, "If I wanted a clown, I would have gone to the circus." Roy didn't try that one again, but he remembers his years at Forest with affection.

"Some people say they had problems with Brian Clough, but he was brilliant to me. We got to Wembley three times during my three years at Forest. We lost to United in the 1992 Rumbelows Cup Final when Choccy scored the winner, and Tottenham in the 1991 FA Cup Final which was awful. I did get a Zenith Data Systems Cup medal though."

Roy's fiery midfield play soon won him a call from the Republic Of Ireland. One typically dynamic Keane performance against Spain in 1993 drew praise from none other than Diego Maradona. "There was no one to touch Roy Keane in that game. I was impressed with everything he did," commented the Argentine superstar.

Naturally, when Forest got relegated in 1993, clubs queued up to sign Roy. "I was desperate to sign Roy for three years", recalls Alex Ferguson. "I never stopped phoning Forest trying to buy him since seeing him on his Forest debut. I said to myself, 'Manchester United must get him.'"

But United might have missed out but for the Keane family loyalties. "United left it a bit late. I'd already spoken to Blackburn and agreed terms, but when I went home to Cork that summer everyone was pressuring me to join United. All my friends and family follow them and I just couldn't say no! Since I joined, they come to visit all the time. They say they want to see how I'm getting on, but I reckon it's just an excuse to see United play!"

For all his success since joining United, Keano's aggressive style of play usually brings him boos from opposing fans. Roy knows that he often walks a tightrope on the pitch. "Aggression has always been part of my game. The ball's there to be won and I wouldn't be doing my job if I was holding back all the time. It's all right being skilful but you've got to have the will to win. I do

need to be a bit more disciplined though and I'm trying to cut down on the silly yellow cards."

In February 1997, Keane was given the United captain's armband for vital League games at Arsenal and Chelsea when Eric Cantona was suspended. At the time, Roy thought it was a doddle: "The only difference is you have to organise the tickets for the lads and go up for the coin toss before the kick-off. At United, there's 11 captains on the pitch. We all know what we've got to do."

Described by Peter Schmeichel as "our most influential player during the 1996/97 season," Roy was the natural choice to take over as captain when Eric retired. As

one of the few brave enough to shout at Cantona when he had made a mistake, Roy doesn't think his new job will affect his play. "I've always shouted at the other lads on the pitch, even before I became captain," smiles Roy, "but I like to think of it as constructive criticism."

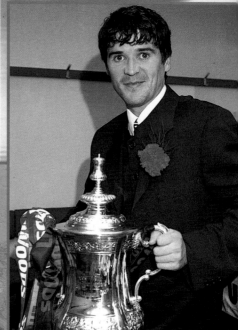

> ## "Fame hasn't changed him a bit. He's still the same as when he left Cork – he's no hell-raiser"
> ### PAT KEANE
> ### Roy's brother

KEANO'S GLOSS FINISH

**v Middlesbrough (a),
23 November 1996**

From the left hand edge of the box, Eric fires the ball towards Becks. David crosses it first time into the middle.

SUITS YOU

Ever wondered what the players do with the suit they wear to Wembley FA Cup Final days? Well, Roy has been to three Cup Finals since he joined United, and he doesn't let them go to gather mothballs in his wardrobe. "I usually give the suit to my Dad or brothers after the game, so they can wear it when they go out."

NO FRILLS

Roy is no poser and he doesn't go in for complicated hairsyling. Keano likes to get a number two all over, let it grow for a few months until it's long and curly and then have it all chopped off again. "The other lads give me stick," smiles Roy "but they love themselves too much anyway. I couldn't care less. I just go out there and play football – that's what I'm paid to do."

SSSSHHHH!

Keep it quiet, but Roy's childhood hero wasn't Captain Courageous Bryan Robson, but Spurs skillster Glenn Hoddle. "Spurs were my team at the time," admits Roy. "I

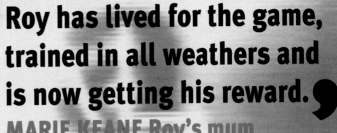

" Roy has lived for the game, trained in all weathers and is now getting his reward. "

MARIE KEANE Roy's mum

think I just supported them to be awkward, as everyone else in Ireland supported United."

HANGING TOUGH

Keano doesn't mind taking the hard knocks to help United win. "He's played with 101 injuries in games for me", says Alex Ferguson. "He's got something in his make-up like Mark Hughes and Bryan Robson had, that no matter what, he'll find a way."

Keano himself reckons it's the thrill of the game that pushes him through the pain barrier: "Once the game starts and the adrenalin flows, you soon forget about any niggling injuries you might have. But people don't see me moaning and groaning, trying to get out of bed the next day!"

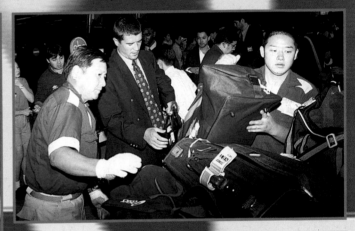

SONGS FOR KEANO

Roy's 110% performances on the pitch have inspired the Old Trafford regulars to dream up some tuneful ditties in tribute to Roy...

"La, La,La,La... La,La, La, La... Hey, Hey... **Keano**
(to the tune of the old Bananarama hit)

"Keano is magic, He wears a magic hat, And when he saw

Old Trafford, He said I fancy that..."

"Boom, Boom, Boom, Everybody say Keano, KEANO!

(to the tune of the Outhere Brothers hit record)

Roy leaps like a salmon and powers a header past Gary Walsh. You know when you've been Keano'd!

PHIL NEVILLE

Debut: v China, 23 May 1996
Caps: 4

"Now there are so many of us United lads in the England squad, it's great. We stick together, eat at the same tables and look out for each other. We never thought we were something special though. "I don't like it when people say Gary and I are the new Charltons. When you think that Bobby won 106 caps, Jack won 35 caps and they won the World Cup, we've got a long way to go."
Phil Neville

"Phil's got pace, he can play either flank. Technically Phil's a very good player and he has taken to the wing-back spot brilliantly. He had never played there for United and that says a lot at this level."
Glenn Hoddle

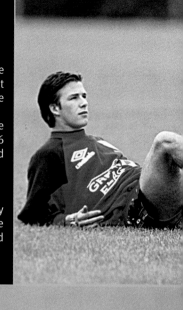

GARY NEVILLE

Debut: v Japan, 3 June 1995
Caps: 22

"I thought I was having my leg pulled when I was first picked for England. It was great working with the likes of Paul Gascoigne. Phil and I watched him on TV at Italia '90 and now we train and play with him. I feel proud every time I play for England. There is such competition for England places that if you miss just one game, you might never be selected again. It means that you always give your best."
Gary Neville

"I remember he came into the United side during a difficult time in 1995 and as a young player dealt with it really well. He had the sort of attitude I really admired." Terry Venables

"As far as I am concerned, Gary is England's best full back." Phil Neville

NICKY BUTT

Debut: v Mexico, 29 March 1997
Caps: 2

"I felt a bit overtaken by Becks, Gary and Phil. They were my mates so I was really pleased for them, but I realised I just had to wait for my chance so I was really pleased to be picked. I was very proud to play for England for the first time. It was great for me to get involved with the squad, working with a lot of exceptional players. I found the game a lot faster than the Premiership, but I felt confident."

£46-million men

England have to insure all club players in their care. Figures are based on their estimated transfer fee and 100 weeks of wages. This is how the FA value United's young lions.

David Beckham £15m
Paul Scholes £8m
Gary Neville £8m
Phil Neville £8m
Nicky Butt £7m

DAVID BECKHAM
Debut: v Moldova, September 1996
Caps: 9

"Alex Ferguson told me I'd been picked and it was an unbelievable feeling. There had been some speculation in the papers, so I was hoping, but not expecting it. I admired Glenn Hoddle a lot as a player; to be picked in his squad was a dream."
David Beckham

"I first came across David in 1995 when I took Chelsea to Old Trafford. I earmarked him as a great talent and he has come on since then, so I had to include him in my first England squad. He's going to be the king-pin."
Glenn Hoddle

YOUNG LIONS

"The beauty of Manchester United is that they are the best team in the country and full of English youngsters. In this day and age, with all the foreigners that have come in, that has got to be a fantastic boost for the English game."
GLENN HODDLE

PAUL SCHOLES
Debut: v South Africa, 24 May 1997
Caps 3

"I don't usually get nervous anyway, but it helped that my debut game was at Old Trafford. I didn't want to swap shirts at the end because it was my first and I wanted to keep it for myself."
Paul Scholes

"Paul has done brilliantly. I always knew he would. It's temperament, you see. It's nothing to do with experience. If you have the temperament to play for United, you have it to play for England."
Gary Neville

"Paul has emerged as one of the big stars. He has looked at home among experienced internationals since he joined us. If Paul can continue as he started, I might really have found a great player."
Glenn Hoddle

"It's a tribute to United's coaching staff that there are five of us with full caps now who have come through the youth system. It's exciting that we can all come together and play for England. We are like young veterans." **GARY NEVILLE**

"Things have settled down for me since I missed playing a few games for Ireland in 1996. I haven't really thought of captaining Ireland. We have a good captain in Andy Townsend, even though he's 54 now!"
ROY KEANE

"It's good for Norwegian football that there are so many of us over here. It makes the national team better and earns the Norwegian game more recognition in Europe. We don't play nice, pretty football, but I think we've changed a little bit. We don't knock long balls all the time now, and we've also got better forwards than we had in '94. Including Ole Gunnar Solskjaer, of course." **HENNING BERG**

FOR CLUB AND

United is a cosmopolitan club – there are eight different nationalities to add flavour to the Reds' first-team squad. Sheringham, Poborsky, Solskjaer, Cruyff and co get together each week and give their all for United, but there's no greater honour for a footballer than representing his country...

"Winning the European Championship with Denmark in 1992 was the greatest moment of my career. Even now I cannot believe I was a European Champion."
PETER SCHMEICHEL

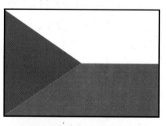

"I made a name for myself in Euro '96, but it's possible that, if I'm not playing full games every week, the Czech manager suspects it will affect my form for the national team. Czech football was on a high after Euro '96 and some people got quite big-headed about it. It was such a good showcase. Although our results have slipped, the feeling of pride is still there among our fans.'
KAREL POBORSKY

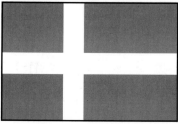

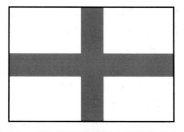

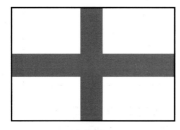

"He's had his critics, but he has come out the other side a better player. He is a far better all-round player now. Cole is part of my plans for the future." HODDLE on COLE

"He is an outstanding player, very clever and subtle. He knows when to drop off and when to join the attack. He is like Gianfranco Zola without the fireworks."
HODDLE on TEDDY SHERINGHAM

"Teddy has got an extra two yards in his head."
SHEARER on SHERINGHAM

COUNTRY

"I'm Welsh through and through. I was born in Wales, so were my mum and dad and my grandparents. I never considered playing for England. Apparently, Terry Venables said to the Boss that he couldn't believe I had been allowed to slip through the English net and play for Wales. It's flattering, but it was always going to be Wales for me. I love playing for my country. It's not often you get the chance to do something for your country, so you've got to make the most of it. It makes me enormously proud, even more so than playing for Manchester United."
RYAN GIGGS

"I'll be at the World Cup, I'm almost sure of that, if I can just get enough games for United. That is the only thing which worries me. At the moment, my club is more important than my country because if you don't perform with the club, you don't have a country."
JORDI CRUYFF

"Ole Gunnar has been a great success, but I believe he has more to offer, season after season."
ALEX FERGUSON

GUN
S

OLE GUNNAR SOLSKJAER

"Ole Gunnar who?" was the response of most United fans when the unknown Norwegian arrived at Old Trafford last summer. One year later, after his goals lead United to another Premiership title, he was being hailed as the finest United goalscorer for 25 years.

While Reds fans were expecting the arrival of Alan Shearer during the summer of 1996, Alex Ferguson quietly went and bought Ole Gunnar Solskjaer from Norwegian side Molde FK for £1.5 million. At a 10th of the price of Shearer, Ferguson even secured one of the all-time great football bargains.

"He's a long-term buy" said Alex Ferguson as he announced his new signing, but Ole Gunnar managed to prove Fergie wrong in his first season by taking his chance immediately. Just six minutes into his debut, on as a sub against Blackburn, Ole Gunnar scored his first goal for United. In his first League start he scored against Nottingham Forest, then on his Champions' League debut against Rapid Vienna he scored again. He went on to become United's leading scorer for the 1996/97 season, with 19 goals.

"I never thought I would get the chance so quickly," says Ole Gunnar. "When my transfer to Manchester United was completed I set myself a target, but I was way off the mark. I hoped to get in the side around Christmas and then get 10 to 15 matches under my belt.

"It was incredible to go from my first club, FK Clausenengen, to United so quickly. They are so different. Clausenengen got small crowds, but I was never

snapped him up for £15,000 in December 1994.

"At FK Clausenengen, I didn't really think about having a professional career at all," he claims. "I was hoping to possibly play in the Norwegian First Division or Premiership maybe. When I got the opportunity at Molde, I found that I could play at that level and score goals." In Ole Gunnar's only full season with Molde, his 20 goals propelled them to the runners-up spot behind Rosenborg.

His form for Molde earned him an international call-up in November 1995 against Jamaica. Naturally, he marked his debut with a goal. Solskjaer began to be known as a promising striker and Italian side Caligari came close to signing him last year. Then United began tracking him, with Chief United scout Les Kershaw attending Molde's game against Lillestrom in May. Reserves manager Jim Ryan also went to watch Ole Gunnar in a World Cup qualifier against Azerbaijan and must have been impressed to see him score twice. In typically modest fashion, Ole Gunnar says, "I knew there was a United scout at the game, but I didn't think he was watching me."

"Yes, Yes, Yes" was his response when he received the call to say United were interested. "There was no way I would say no. It was a wonderful feeling to join them.

"Life has been smiling on me," reflects Ole on his meteoric rise. "Ten years ago I only dreamed about playing abroad."

So how does Ole Gunnar explain his success? "I find it natural to score goals. It's being in the right place at the right time. When I head towards goal, which I have done many times, I know exactly what to

"I first saw Ole Gunnar when he was 19. His finishing and general skills were superb already. After less than 10 minutes of training, I realised he was destined for big things."
AAGE HAREIDE, MANAGER OF MOLDE FK

do." And from his debut goal against Blackburn to his match-saving double at Leicester, his goals helped United to another title. Old Trafford embraced Ole Gunnar; the song sung with the most passion during the 1996/97 season was

scared of playing at Old Trafford. This is what football's all about. I've always dreamt about playing in front of big crowds. When the crowd sings 'Ole, Ole, Ole', it really lifts me and gives me more confidence."

Ole Gunnar was nearly lost to a career in wrestling thanks to the influence of his father, a seven-time Norwegian wrestling champion: "My father tried to make me a wrestler, but I didn't like it," says the striker. "For two years I trained and I was getting thrown all over the place, so I thought this isn't my sport!"

Ole Gunnar broke into his local team, Clausenengen, in 1991 and went on to score 86 goals in just four years there. In his last season he amassed 31 goals, the highest number in that League for 20 years. Such prolific goal scoring attracted Norwegian Premiership side Molde FK, who

"You are my Solskjaer... "
The amount of Norwegian press coverage Ole Gunnar receives is enormous. Not a

He works very hard and scores very important
Jean-Pierre Papin because he is t

OLE
GOAL
POWER
v Sunderland (h)
21 December 1996

Ole Gunnar's second goal in this 5–0 thrashing of Sunderland demonstrated the young Norwegian's devastating

single day passes without a mention of him in the two biggest Oslo tabloid newspapers. English football is incredibly popular in Norway and the Norwegian tabloids have correspondents based in Britain with one purpose: to cover Norwegians in the Premiership. Solskjaer is the main attraction.

But Ole Gunnar is genuinely modest about his success. "Last season was something of an apprenticeship," he says. "There was so much to learn from my team-mates and the coaching staff. They are largely responsible for my success. I don't have the talent of Giggs or Beckham, so I compensate for the lack of natural ability by watching what I eat, drink and generally do in life. I can't afford to be careless with what I have got."

When United won the Premiership in May, some United players were collecting their fourth Championship medal, but it was a new experience for Ole Gunnar. "It was the first time I've won anything in football, apart from an Under-11 or Under-12 district

championship. That Tuesday was wonderful. I was sat in front of my telly and watched West Ham versus Newcastle and Wimbledon's clash with Liverpool. Ronny called just after the final whistle – we stood there screaming to each other like madmen. It was marvellous. And I want more of that wonderful feeling."

SONG FOR SOLSKJAER
You are my Solskjaer,
My Ole Solskjaer,
You make me happy
When skies are grey,
Oh Alan Shearer,
He might be dearer,
But please don't take
My Solskjaer away.

OLE OF ME

1 Nicknames?
The lads just call me Ollie. You pronounce Ole, Ooo-le, and my full name is Ole Gunnar, but I don't mind how they say it.

2 Fave music?
I like rock music. I went to see Sting with Eric, Ronny and Peter. He's not my favourite artist but I enjoyed the concert.

3 Lingo?
I speak three: Norwegian, English and bit of German.

4 Chef talents?
I can make a good Norwegian salmon dish.

5 Reading?
I liked *Cantona On Cantona* and Alex Ferguson's diary, which was very good. I read a lot of football books and Norwegian newspapers.

6 First pair of football boots?
I remember my father cutting the rubbers off some of his shoes and glueing them on to mine! That was when I was about three years old.

7 Skiing?
Cross country skiing is popular in Norway. I used to ski a lot during the winter, especially in the Christmas holidays.

8 Top TV programmes?
I usually watch Sky Sports, or Norwegian channels, so I don't watch *Eastenders*! The best programme is *Seinfeld*. It's a comedy. I also watch a lot of videos, mostly in English.

9 Bad habits?
You will have to ask Ronny that one.

10 Fave magazines?
I read football magazines like *Manchester United Magazine* and *Glory Glory Man United*. I also enjoy *FourFourTwo* and *Goal*. Back in Norway, I used to buy *Shoot* and *Match* every week.

❝ Ole is very important to Manchester United.
s. He is good, very good, and he reminds me so much of
me type of exciting, energetic player. ❞ ERIC CANTONA

pace, and cool finishing. Having run half the length of the pitch, Ole left goalie Perez doing the splits in despair.

Room mates

During the season, footballers live out of a suitcase. For the average away Premiership fixture, the United players travel down the day before the game; for Champions' League matches, they will fly into Europe a couple of days in advance of kick-off. Because the lads spend so much time together in hotels, it's important to find the right room-mate. Some like to swap around a bit: David Beckham has shared with Ben Thornley, Gary Neville and Teddy during the past year. Others, like Roy Keane and Denis Irwin, can't be separated. The team spirit at United is good, but some players have their little quirks which can make even an easy-going roomie go mad. Here's the insider guide to Red life in the bedroom...

Time share:
Becks, Pally, Ryan and Andy relax in Porto

Nicky Butt on Paul Scholes
"Paul's a good mate, but a bad room-mate. He stays up late and watches TV and then falls asleep so I have to get up at 2 am to turn it off. Then in the morning, he gets up dead early, puts the light on, turns on the TV and rustles the newspapers. I would never do anything like that if someone was asleep!"

Ole Gunnar Solskjaer on Ronny Johnsen
"I knew Ronny from the Norwegian national team before I joined United. When I first got here I relied on him a lot. I like rooming with him because we speak to each other in our own language. We can both speak good English, but Norwegian is easier!"

Karel Poborsky on Brian McClair
"I quite appreciate Brian's humour... and he has helped me a tremendous amount with my English."

ROOM

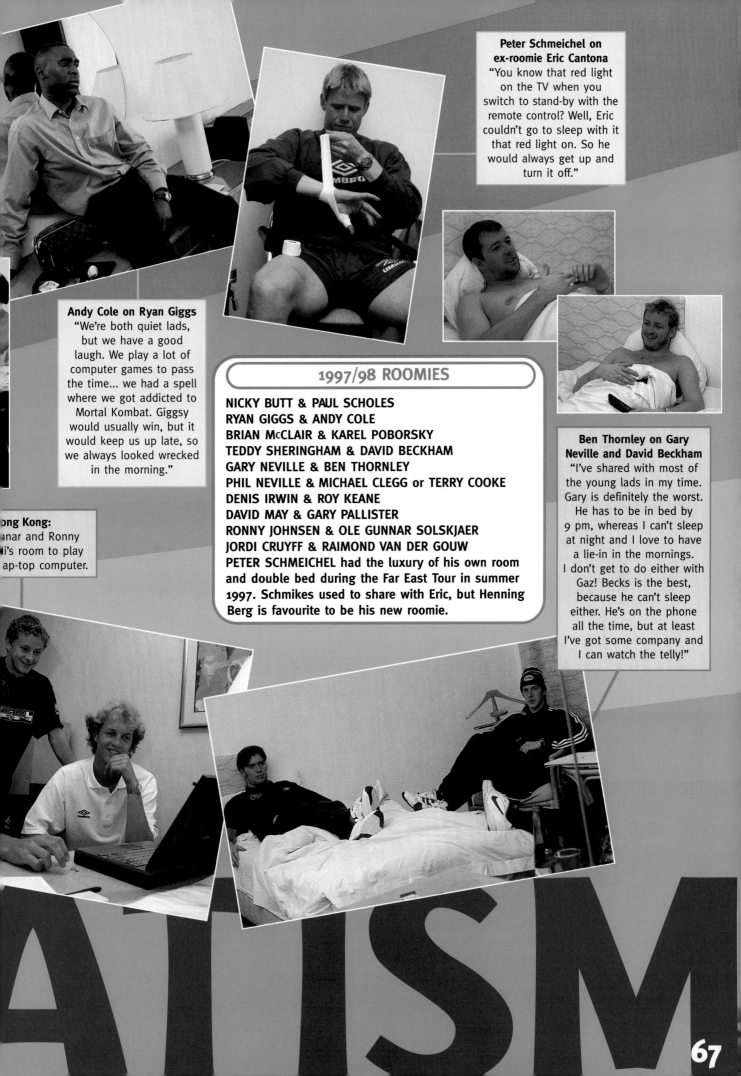

1997/98 ROOMIES

NICKY BUTT & PAUL SCHOLES
RYAN GIGGS & ANDY COLE
BRIAN McCLAIR & KAREL POBORSKY
TEDDY SHERINGHAM & DAVID BECKHAM
GARY NEVILLE & BEN THORNLEY
PHIL NEVILLE & MICHAEL CLEGG or TERRY COOKE
DENIS IRWIN & ROY KEANE
DAVID MAY & GARY PALLISTER
RONNY JOHNSEN & OLE GUNNAR SOLSKJAER
JORDI CRUYFF & RAIMOND VAN DER GOUW
PETER SCHMEICHEL had the luxury of his own room and double bed during the Far East Tour in summer 1997. Schmikes used to share with Eric, but Henning Berg is favourite to be his new roomie.

HE SCOF

The great Manchester United youth teams of the early Nineties included Beckham, the Nevilles and Butt. However, most fans came to watch the Salford boy they dubbed "young Cantona". Now, Paul Scholes is set to wear Eric's crown...

Cheeky chappy

Two good feet?

"I'll sit this one out"

SCHOLES MEANZ GOALS

v Swindon Town (h)
23 October 1996

Scholesy receives the ball in a tight spot on the edge of Swindon's area. Two defenders surround him but Paul

ES GOALS...

EARLY PROMISE

"When Paul Scholes played in the junior sides, he used to have his own personal fan club of people who came just to watch him play. When I first clapped eyes on him, it was just like watching Kenny Dalglish in his prime. I honestly believed that Paul had every chance of becoming a top-class striker. He had the craft, intelligence, vision and that vital acceleration over five yards."
YOUTH TEAM COACH, ERIC HARRISON

"Our school played a team from Altrincham in the 1986 Catholic Schools Cup Final. Paul was just 12 and tiny in comparison to our opponents, but a giant on the field. Paul ran the midfield, they couldn't touch him. He could strike the ball perfectly with hardly any backlift. It was sheer timing and skill. We won 3–1, thanks mainly to Paul, and went on to win the Cup three times in the next four years."
JOHN DURCAN, headmaster, Cardinal Langley RC School, Middleton

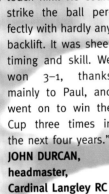
Fledgling talent

"He had skill and vision, and his final touch was amazing. None of the other lads could get the ball off him – he just bamboozled them."
MICHAEL COFFEY, Paul's school team coach and official United scout

SICK NOTE

For years, Scholesy's career suffered because of a mystery illness affecting his form during the winter months. "I used to get five or six bad colds every winter," remembers Paul. "I'd get short of breath during matches and feel tired all the time. It was really frustrating. But I went to see a specialist in 1996 who told me it was a minor form of asthma. He gave me an inhaler, and I got through winter without a problem. Touch wood, that's the end of it."

TWO GOOD FEET?

Fergie has often said that Paul has got 'two excellent feet'. Paul disagrees. "If there is one thing I'd change about my appearance, it would be my feet. They're horrible – it's their shape and the smell!"

GINGER SNAPS

1 Match nerves?
"You can't allow yourself to get nervous. You have to concentrate on the game, and although you enjoy hearing the crowd, you can't let it intimidate you."

2 Club nickname?
"A few call me 'Ging' but most call me Scholesy."

3 Best advice?
"Remember, your best friends are the bottom of your boots, your studs!"

4 Hard nut?
"I don't see myself as hard. I try to play honestly and I'm not the kind of player who will stay down for no reason."

5 Pet hates?
"People who drive very slowly. I hate traffic, waiting at the lights, anything."

11 stone on the button

MY DEBUT

**v Port Vale (a), 2–1
21 September 1994**

"For my first goal, I intercepted a bad pass from their left back. Luckily I got to it before the covering defender, put it through his legs and just chipped the keeper. It hit the post and

went in. For the second goal, I just remember the cross coming over from Simon Davies and my header just got a nick off the bloke's head jumping with me, which guided it in the corner. It was a shock next morning to wake up and see my name in the headlines – 'Scholes Boy Hero' and all that. Yeah, I always wanted to play for United, but you can't think about headlines and all that. I just wanted to play football."

Three days after this double strike, Paul proved it was no fluke by scoring on his League debut, 11 minutes after coming on as sub v Ipswich Town.

THE FUTURE:
"I don't waste time dreaming. That doesn't mean I don't care. I'm very determined to be here and want to be playing in 10 year's time." PAUL SCHOLES

turns on a sixpence and his missile cross-shot smashes in off the post. Another Scholes scorcher!

TOUGH COOKIE

It is a testament to Nicky Butt's stature at United that when Paul Ince came on the market in the summer of 1997, United did not even consider exercising the first option they held to buy. Quite understandable when you consider that, since Ince's surprise departure in 1995, Butt has helped United to two Championships, an FA Cup and broken into the England squad...

Cup of cheer

"Harry McShane spotted me when I was playing for Droylsden," says Nicky, "He used to come and watch us, then Brian Kidd came along and I was invited down for trials. I signed as a schoolboy and it just went on from there."

"What a handful he was in those days!" remembers Eric Harrison. "He wanted to fight everyone on the other side. I told him that he might win his battles at this level but he wouldn't get away with it in the Premiership."

"When you start out at 16, your eyes are

to fend for yourself. When you get a professional contract, you think 'I've got a permanent job now for x amount of years.' That's the main aim."

Nicky was part of the great class of '92 Youth team, which included the Nevilles, Beckham, Scholes and Giggs. Together they were responsible for United's first FA Youth Cup win since 1964. "Winning the Cup was great, especially as it was only the first year of our apprenticeship," Butt recalls. "It was brilliant because most of the lads were first years. They were good times.

> ## "He is without doubt one of the bravest players I have ever come across in all my time at Old Trafford. He is the one you want by your side when the going gets tough."
> ERIC HARRISON

My belief in Nicky was essential to our decision to sell Paul Ince," says Alex Ferguson. "I always thought he could blossom like he has. I had every confidence in him as a player."

While some of Nicky's team-mates might receive bigger headlines, Nicky has few peers in the middle of the field where the ball needs to be won. Not many opponents get past him: during the 1996/97 season, Nicky was successful in 79% of his tackles. With Roy Keane, he forms the most feared midfield partnership in the Premiership.

wide open, looking at all the first-team lads who are your heroes," recalls Nicky. "You're in a big club, you meet new people and all of a sudden you've got big responsibilities. You get your wage, you pay your mum this, that and the other, and you're thrown straight into the big world, and you've got

Happy daze

Nicky Butt is one o

BUTTY DAZZLER

v Leicester City (h)
30 November 1996

Nick played a one-two with Cantona, chesting Eric's return pass on to his right foot before flicking the ball past

A lot of the lads are still at United of course, but we still speak quite a bit to the ones who aren't."

Nicky made his debut in November 1992, as a substitute for Paul Ince against Oldham – a sign of things to come. He had to wait a further two years before he made a more permanent breakthrough into the first team, during the 1994/95 season. "All the games I thought I played well that season, we lost!" He is right, but it was nothing to be ashamed of. Against Barcelona in the intimidating Nou Camp and in the Cup Final against Everton, Butt was United's best player.

With Ince's departure in the summer of 1995, Nicky was handed a regular place and responded by helping United to the Double. "You look back now and think of all the great teams that have won Doubles, and then you think 'I was part of one.' It's excellent to have done that, but you can't dwell on it. We want to go further and win as many trophies as we can, and do better than anybody who's ever been at this club.

"I became stronger that season, but also I think my knowledge of the game at the top level improved. I understand it better and know what to do and when to do it. When I was younger, I just kept running forward all the time without really thinking about the defensive part. Now I realise you can't do that because you leave big gaps; you have to do it when the time is right."

Manchester United fans don't need to worry about our Nicky leaving the club. "I am a Manchester lad and love it up here, I'd hate to live in London. If I was offered double the money, I wouldn't move down there."

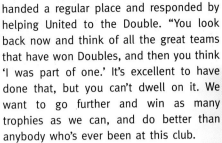
One of the lads

hatch slurp

Park life

"Wahey!"

Pawn to E5

ey figure for United now and heir best players. " PAUL INCE

a bamboozled defender. Quick as a flash, Nicky finished the job with a rasping left-foot shot. Just Butt-iful!

A professional career at United is a great life. You get paid to play the game you love, you stay super-fit, 55,000 people cheer you on every few days and you have your afternoons off. Here's a leisurely guide to the Reds relaxing in their spare time...

Nicky juggles three

Trivial Pursuits

● In Vienna last year, Maysie and Pally beat Eric and Schmikes in a table football/pool challenge The defensive duo's chant of "2–0 to the Champions" could be heard all around the team hotel after their triumph.

● Phil Neville had the ability to play cricket for England if he hadn't chosen a career in football. Andy Cole was also a useful cricketer and was offered a district trial... but he didn't turn up. Gary Pallister has also been known to flourish the willow in charity games.

● When United stayed at the Oakley Court Hotel near Windsor before the 1997 Charity Shield match, there was plenty of action in the snooker room. Giggsy proved to be king of the green baize. "Ryan's got a natural eye" reports our insider spy. "He just gets down and pots them."

● Manager Alex Ferguson and coach Brian Kidd make sure that the players rest their legs between training and matches during the season. "There are times when the players are told not to do things like play golf or even go shopping," says Brian. "Fortunately, we have a very professional bunch of lads here and they know the standards we expect."

● A game of cards is a popular time-filler for Pally, Keano, Teddy, Nicky, Maysie and Paul Scholes on away trips – Brag and Hearts are their favourite games.

Ryan loses his head

Two crazy golfers

Teddy takes the rest

Maysie plays with his pet rotweiler Ronny

Teddy hits the road

Peter zooms in

Arguments rage over who is the world's best striker, midfielder or defender. But the world's best goalkeeper? No contest. Peter Schmeichel. In his six years at Old Trafford, Schmeichel has developed his reputation as the world's best by helping Manchester United dominate English football and inspiring the small nation of Denmark to European Championship victory.

PETER SCHMEICHEL

"There's no doubt in my mind. Schmeichel's the number one in Europe and probably the world right now," says Alex Ferguson. "He has everything he needs to dominate, with that presence great goalkeepers have. Peter is lightning quick and brave as a lion.

"It's his entire aura, this big, blond Viking flying out at you. It cuts an attacker's options down 10 times. He has added bits to his game as the years have passed, but the one that has never changed is that Peter is a winner. To me, that's his most important feature. It takes him days to get over a defeat, and there are not many Europeans like that."

"My heart is here at Old Trafford," says the most successful keeper in United's history. "This is the best team with the best fans and the best manager in football. We are capable of winning anything we set our minds to. I like to win things, so I want to be part of it."

The young Peter actually wanted to play at the other end of the pitch. "At my first proper training session, when I was nine, I played as a striker, but my coach wasn't too impressed with

my early touches as an outfield player! I was a bit too wild. He asked me to keep goal instead and that's what I've done ever since.

"When you're a kid, anything is possible. As I got older and better, I started to believe that I could actually make the grade as a goalkeeper. I put a lot of pressure on myself and worked and trained like a madman. I think I had a certain talent, even from the early days. And I've had quality coaching along the way."

"I used to dream about playing for United, even though I was thousands of miles away. They were always my favourite club. I liked Gary Bailey – more because of the colour of his hair than anything. I could see myself in goal for United, being blond myself!"

Peter began his career at the small Danish club Hvidore. After two years, he moved on to Denmark's top club Brondby, where he won three Championships and was voted Denmark's Player of the Year in 1990. His reputation spread rapidly across Europe.

United's manager Alex Ferguson asked Alan Hodgkinson, his goalkeeping coach, to watch Peter over six games at international and club

THE GREATEST SAVE EVER!

IT MATCHED MINE SAYS BANKSIE

> ## "I can't believe this! I get all the blame for shouting. The truth is that they shout at me more than I shout at them. Even Butty and Keano – they're all at it."

level. Hodgkinson's report was simple and to the point: "Schmeichel is the best goalkeeper in Europe." Ferguson acted quickly and signed him for a mere £500,000. "At that price for a goalkeeper, I believe we made the buy of the century," said Ferguson.

Manchester United had been without a reliable presence between the posts since Alex Stepney was at his peak nearly two decades earlier. The lack of silverware was not just a coincidence. In his very first season Peter conceded only 33 goals, the lowest in the League. And he kept up that standard.

In the summer of 1992, as a late replacement in the European Championship for war-torn Yugoslavia, Denmark and Peter stunned the football world by winning the tournament. With his inspired performances against Germany and Holland, Peter became a national hero. "It was the greatest day of my footballing career," he says of the final. "I hope there will be many others to come. Even now I can't believe I'm a European champion."

Throughout his United career, Peter has maintained his record of conceding less than a goal a game. Such goalkeeping has been the foundation of United's ascendancy in the Nineties. Eric Cantona may be referred to as the catalyst for United's success, but Peter

has been just as important. "People believe Eric Cantona won us the Premiership in 1995/96, and it's true that his form from January to the end of the season was unbelievable," says Alex Ferguson. "But Peter's contribution was just as great. He was making great saves when the score was 0–0 or 1–0 to us. We had eight 1–0 victories, so it was that as much as anything that helped us win that title. He saves ten to twelve points that other keepers are not getting."

England World Cup winner Gordon Banks, who knows a bit about goalkeeping, is

also a fan. "Schmeichel's great strength is that he dominates his area like no other British goalkeeper. They seem happy to hug the goal-line, which is no good. Schmeichel is off his line and ready, so when

> ## ❝It was as good as mine against Pelé. Peter had to get lower than I did. It was a magnificent save. One of the best I've seen. ❞
>
> ### GORDON BANKS, ENGLAND'S 1966 WORLD CUP GOALIE

THE ONE THAT GOT AWAY...

v Wimbledon (a)
4 February 1997

With United 1–0 down and just minutes remaining of this FA Cup tie, the Great Dane went up for a United corner.

SCHMIKES' SEVEN

1 England?
My family likes living in England, but home is home, and when I finish my playing career we will move back to Denmark

2 Fave TV?
Harry Enfield and Chums, *Men Behaving Badly*, *Absolutely Fabulous*, *TFI Friday*... the Brits are definitely world champs at making television!

3 First pair of boots?
They had no brand name, they were just a pair of plastic football boots

4 How many boots a season?
I maybe go through two pairs of match boots in a season. The boots we wear in a game are not used for training, so you don't need to change match boots quite so often

5 Superstitions?
I kick each goal post before each half of the match. I have done that all my life and I have lost a lot of games as well, but I still do it

6 Music?
When I come back home after a game, I play the piano or my drums to unwind. It's very relaxing for me. I released my own single, "We Can Do It Again", in Denmark. I played the guitar and drums and did a little rap. It was a smash hit and all the litle kids in Denmark were singing it!

7 Most prized possession?
My contract with United! Also I received a small replica Premiership trophy when we won the first Premiership in 1993, instead of the normal winners' medal. I'm quite proud to be one of only 14 players ever to receive that prize

---

he's called upon he's already halfway there."

Peter may well be a frustrated striker, but he compensates by getting involved in forward play with his attack-launching throws. "If I see the opportunity to release an attacker, I will throw the ball because it is so much more accurate than kicking it," he explains. "Those throws are outstanding," says Ferguson. "They are like Glenn Hoddle's passes, taking out half a dozen opponents in one go. His distribution is fantastic."

Many can't understand Peter's constant bawling out of his team mates but, he says, it is integral to his game. "Shouting is my weapon to stay aware. Not a lot happens at my end of the field, but it's important to be part of the match. The lads shout at me too, but the cameras always point my way! I think

it helps. If I make a mistake, Pally and Maysie will tell me and I'll make sure I don't make it next time. I do the same for them too."

Even Schmeichel managed to outdo himself in 1996 in Vienna. In the crucial Champions' League clash against Rapid Vienna, he saved a header from Rene Wagner that appeared to have already gone past him. So great was the save that the next day's newspapers compared it to Gordon Banks' amazing save from Pelé in the 1970 World Cup.

Peter has 14 medals from six years at United, but he won't be resting on his laurels. "I'm a proud goalkeeper and it's never fun to concede a goal. Every time I let one in, I look at myself to see if there was anything I could have done. You can't go through life just saying, 'I don't make mistakes.'"

KITTED OUT

Schmikes is United kit man Albert Morgan's worst nightmare. The following items must be in the number one's place on the dressing room bench before every game...

- A pair of socks and shorts, plus a sweat top for the warm-up
- Two pairs of briefs
- Four undershirts
- A pair of elbow pads
- A back belt
- Waterproofs
- Two pairs of boots

- A pair of flip-flops (for walking around in the dressing room)
- Two match shirts
- A pair of match shorts
- A pair of brand-new match socks for every game
- Two pairs of goalkeeping gloves

Albert keeps a spare set of everything in his kitbag for all the players, in case of emergencies. So when Denis Irwin's shorts were ripped off during the Middlesbrough game in May 1997, Albert jumped off the bench to spare Den's blushes!

Schmikes, lurking in the six-yard box, launched an amazing scissors kick sending the fans wild. But he was offside!

SPEAKEASY

"I can remember the boss bringing Beckham into the changing room a couple of times whenever we played in London. The gaffer would introduce him to all the players, show him around. When Dave'd gone he would curse the fact that he hadn't signed for us yet. David wasn't shy then and he isn't now but he can't understand why the papers are fascinated by his private life. My reply to that is, 'Well don't go out with a Spice Girl!'
CHOCCY MCCLAIR on KID BECKHAM

"I don't know who would win a fight between Eric, Keano and Schmikes, but I reckon it would be a good scrap between the three of them!"
MAYSIE on ROY AND PETER

"Nicky Butt is probably my best mate at the club. We went on holiday together last summer with our girlfriends."
SCHOLES on BUTT

"Respect to Becks, he's handled all the attention well. If you start getting a bit out of hand, you soon get knocked down. You get a bit of a hammering!"
BUTT on BECKS

"He's a top bloke, David. Always taking the mickey, good to have a laugh with."
GARY NEV on MAYSIE

"The biggest respect that you can pay Roy Keane is that nobody likes playing against him. He's a competitor, a driving force and he's got a little bit of the devil in him."
PALLY on KEANO

"When things are written in the papers about you, you have to expect the lads to give you some grief. David May is definitely the worst for dishing out stick."
BECKS on MAYSIE

"I just tell him to get his hair cut, but I can't talk because I've been told the same!"
BECKS on POBORSKY

"Becks is always getting the mick taken out of him because he is so flash. He's a typical Cockney with a strong London accent which we're always imitating. He's also has his hair slicked back, so he gets stick for being a pretty boy."
GIGGS on BECKS

"Andy's very quiet when he's with the lads, but I room with him and he's not so quiet when we're in our room. In fact, he's a riot!"
GIGGS on COLE

"He's really easy to wind up. All you have to do is take the mickey out of something you've heard him say. Ryan tries to be very polite in public, always saying, 'thank you' and stuff, but he's definitely not polite to us !"
BUTT on GIGGS

"He is very untidy. If he puts on a clean shirt and decides he doesn't like it he'll throw it down – that can get on my nerves. He also drives too fast, but he's got a clean licence!"
PHIL on BROTHER GARY

"I don't think Phil ever scores a goal, to be honest. He scored one once in the under-elevens! At school he was renowned for scoring own goals!"
GARY on PHIL

"When we play golf or snooker together, I always beat him. He just keeps coming back for more."
PHIL on GARY

See ya later!

OTHER TITLES

available from Manchester United Books

A Will To Win: The Manager's Diary
by Alex Ferguson £14.99
ISBN 0 233 99106 9

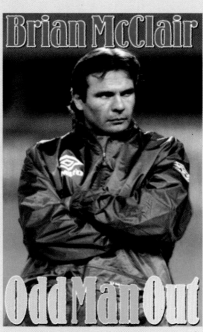

Odd Man Out: A Player's Diary
by Brian McClair £14.99
ISBN 0 233 99115 8

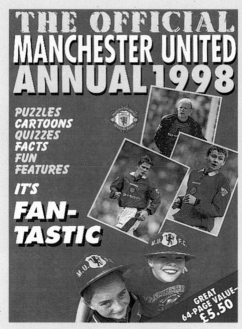

**Manchester United
Annual 1998** £5.50
ISBN 0 233 99164 6

**Manchester United Ultimate
Football File** £5.99
ISBN 0 233 99034 8

**Manchester United in
the Sixties** £12.99
ISBN 0 233 99178 6

**Manchester United 1998
Pocket Diary** £4.99
ISBN 0 233 99220 0

**Manchester United
Little Devils** £4.99
ISBN 0 233 99041 0

ALL THESE BOOKS ARE AVAILABLE AT YOUR LOCAL BOOKSHOP OR CAN BE ORDERED DIRECT FROM THE PUBLISHER. PRICES AND AVAILABLITY ARE SUBJECT TO CHANGE WITHOUT NOTICE.

SEND ORDER TO:
Manchester United Cash Sales, 106 Great Russell Street, London WC1B 3LJ.
Please send a cheque or postal order made payable to André Deutsch Ltd for the value of the book(s) plus postage and packing (see below). Remember to give your name and address.

POSTAGE AND PACKING:
UK: add £1.00 for the first book, 50p for the second and 30p for each additional book up to a a maximum of £3.00.
OVERSEAS *including* EIRE: add £2.00 for the first book, £1.00 for the second and 50p for each additional book up to a maximum of £5.00.